Which Rite
is
Right?

The Eucharistic Prayer
in
The Anglican Tradition

Peter Toon

Preservation Press

P.O. Box 612 • Swedesboro, NJ 08085

Which Rite is Right?

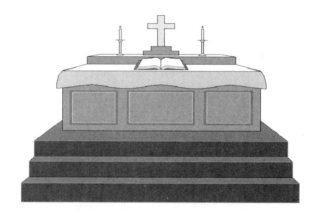

For
Jim and Meg Beales of Chestnut Hill, PA.,

who graciously provided hospitality and transport
for the author during the Fall of 1993, and who
enthusiastically share his commitment to the
Common Prayer Tradition of the Anglican Way.

Contents

CHAPTER ONE

The Anglican Scene

Why do we as human beings exist? As creatures made in the image and after the likeness of the living God, we are alive to enjoy and glorify the Lord our God for ever, unto ages of ages. In private prayer and especially in public worship, we assemble to adore him, to praise him, to give thanks unto him, to offer petitions to him, to intercede on behalf of others and to confess our sins unto him, and to hear his word of pardon and commission. We come to the Father through the Son in the Holy Spirit by grace and thus in humility. We celebrate the mighty words and deeds of the Lord our God, because the Father has come to us in the Son and by the Holy Spirit in revelation and glory in order to save us.

Sunday worship

As a branch of the one, holy, catholic, and apostolic Church of God, the Anglican Church has always taught (though not necessarily practiced!) that on the Lord's Day the Lord's people ought to meet at the Lord's Table in the Lord's House, and there offer spiritual worship in order to enjoy and glorify God. Over the centuries, however, some parishes have made Morning Prayer their primary Sunday service, preferring to have Holy Communion once a month. However, the vast majority of parishes now accept that each Sunday they are called by their Lord to meet together in worship for the ministry of the Word and of the Sacrament. They are to hear the Word of God and receive the sacramental Body and Blood of Christ for the salvation of their souls, as they adore, praise, and thank their God, and as they pray both for themselves and for others.

Once it is accepted that the primary service for the household of faith is the Order for the Administration of Holy Communion, then the question arises, What Order or Rite shall be used? Gone are the days when there was only one Order in any one place and when such a question was not asked. Today, for good or ill, there is choice! Not a few people are confused by this availability of different Rites and Orders printed in a variety of Prayer Books.

The confusion is not only within Episcopal or Anglican parishes, which officially are part of the Anglican Communion. It is amongst the growing body of people who belong to the "continuing Anglican churches" and within those who are on what may be called "the liturgical [or the Canterbury] trail." They are moving out of *ex tempore* services, which depend upon the inspiration and ability of the "worship leader," towards ordered, traditional forms of worship. Yet, as they move they find that the title, *Book of Common Prayer*, is used in America not only of truly "Common Prayer" (one and one only Order or Rite) as in the 1928 *Book of Common Prayer*, but also of modern prayer books (for example the 1979 Book of the Episcopal Church and the 1985 Book of the Canadian Church), which contain a variety of Rites from which a parish can choose one or several.

Therefore, for those who belong to the Episcopal Church in the USA, and who dutifully use the 1979 Prayer Book, there is choice within that book. First of all, there is choice between a traditional and a modern language Rite (Rites One and Two). In the second place, there are two Eucharistic Prayers in Rite One (Options I and II) and four Eucharistic Prayer (Options A,B,C & D) in Rite Two. Certainly all six are made to conform to a general structure, but they remain different in content.

For those who belong to the Continuing Anglican Churches, of which there are possibly up to twenty (mostly very small) jurisdictions in North America, the choice (at least in theory) is even greater. For traditionalists, there are all the major Prayer Books of the Anglican Common Prayer Tradition from 1549 (England) to 1962 (Canada) as well as the Anglican or American Missal; and for those who want modern forms there are all the provisions of the modern Prayer Books produced since the 1970's (e.g., the Australian of 1978, the American of 1979, the English of 1980 and the Canadian of 1985).

In practice, most of the jurisdictions restrict the choice to one or two possibilities (e.g., the American 1928 BCP and the American Missal in the "Anglo-Catholic" Continuing Churches [the ACA, the ACC, the UECNA, the PCK, and the EMC], and the 1979 American Episcopal Book in the Charismatic Episcopal Church).

For those who belong to the Reformed Episcopal Church there used to be no choice. Congregations could only use the official Prayer Book of 1874. Now they are in a period of experimentation and with a bishop's agreement can use the 1928 BCP, the 1662 BCP, and the Australian modern language Prayer Book of 1978. This is a remarkable comprehensiveness for a small denomination. It may also be a source of confusion to members!

To summarize; not only is there the obvious supermarket of denominations, and forms of worship from which Americans who wish to attend church must choose; but there is also a small subdivision of that supermarket called Episcopalianism or Anglicanism. Within this small subdivision, are various denominations and Prayer Books, as well as Rites or Orders for Holy Communion on offer. To be an Anglican one has to choose one or another from the selection. One cannot turn a blind eye to the selection and pretend it does not exist. One needs to know what one is selecting and why.

The purpose

The purpose of this small book is to provide a guide to this small corner of the supermarket of religions. It is to present and explain this variety of Rites or Orders in historical and theological context. More particularly, it is to examine the Prayers of Consecration (or the Eucharistic Prayers) within the Rites and to show wherein they agree and how they differ - and for what theological reasons.

In writing, I have had in mind several groups of Anglicans or would-be Anglicans. *First of all,* as a priest of the diocese of Quincy, I address members of the Episcopal Church, who are still ready to look back beyond 1979 for guidance in worship. My recent experience at the General Convention of the ECUSA in Indianapolis (August 1994) taught me that there is a great need for Episcopalians to recover their best liturgical tradition, since they are in great danger of being lost in the raging seas of confused modernity. Some of the liturgies used in public worship at the General Convention were distinctively *modern* (politically correct) rather than being distinctively *Anglican.*

In the second place, I write for the clergy and congregations belonging to the increasingly varied Continuing Anglican Churches (founded since 1976). Not a few of these jurisdictions have kindly invited me to address them. I share their desire to recover authentic Anglicanism as a form of Reformed Catholic Christianity; and I sincerely hope that they will recover it as being dynamically both *evangelical* and *catholic,* both *biblical* and *traditional,* and both being *in the Spirit* and *faithful to a sound orthodoxy.* Within this category, I think particularly of the fastest growing segment, the Charismatic Episcopal Church, many of whose members have only minimal roots in traditional Anglicanism, but who are nevertheless enthusiastic for the Anglican Way. I believe they are interested to know more about Anglican Rites, and I hope that they will be enabled to look beyond the modern Prayer Books into the classic Anglican Tradition for inspiration and guidance.

In the third place, I offer my work to clergy and congregations of the Reformed Episcopal Church (founded 1874). It has been my pleasure to have taught as a visiting professor in its seminary in Philadelphia. This Church, representing an evangelical wing of Anglicanism, is beginning to grow, especially in the South and West. Independent congregations are seeking to be admitted to the care of its bishops and thereby into the Anglican Common Prayer Tradition through this Church.

Finally, I write for those who are on what is often called "the liturgical trail." Some of these are being attracted by the Reformed Episcopal Church, others by the Charismatic Episcopal Church and yet others by the Antiochene Orthodox Church. Even if my book does not persuade them to enter the Anglican fold, I hope that it will give them a good understanding of the Anglican Way in terms of its approach to the Holy Eucharist.

There is nothing original in this book. Its usefulness, I hope, lies in the fact that it brings together, in a readable form, information about Liturgy and Theology which would normally have to be gathered from a variety of sources. The reader will soon realize my own preferences (which are partially explained by the fact that I am a priest of the Church of England), but I hope that my own convictions do not stand in the way of the distilling of correct information and rational comment and interpretation.

In two books, *Knowing God through the Liturgy* (1992) and *Proclaiming the Gospel through the Liturgy* (1993), I have declared my own commitment to the Anglican Way and its classic Common Prayer Tradition. In an earlier book, *The Anglican Way, Evangelical and Catholic,* I commended the Anglican Way as preserving in a dynamic form, the truth of the Gospel in a reformed catholic context.

In the pages which follow, I look into the Common Prayer Tradition in a different way than I did in those three books. My purpose here is to note the excellence, as well as the similarities and differences, with respect to the Eucharist: (a) within the family of Prayer Books of the Common Prayer Tradition, and (b) within those new Prayer Books now associated with, but not, technically speaking, a part of that Common Prayer Tradition.

To set the theological context for the understanding of the Anglican Way in its origins, I provide in the next chapter an introduction to the general approach of sixteenth and seventeenth century Anglicanism to Scripture and Tradition. Then later in the book, before I look at modern liturgies, I provide an introduction to the modern, twentieth-century approach to Scripture and Tradition.

It is my hope that the late 1990s will witness the growing together into unity (at least in terms of intercommunion) of the various groups, churches and denominations which seek to be faithful to the Gospel of the Father concerning the Lord Jesus as biblical and catholic Anglicans. If this book serves to make a contribution to this unity I shall be pleased.

CHAPTER TWO

Scripture, Tradition, and Reason

What has always been true of the Anglican Way of Christianity in its authentic form is its commitment first to Holy Scripture as the final authority for faith and conduct, and secondly, to Tradition as the guide to how Scripture has been received and interpreted in the Church. This approach has been guided by "right reason," and so it has often been said that Anglicanism is committed to Scripture, tradition and reason.

Anyone who examines the formularies (i.e., the Prayer Book, the Ordinal, the Articles of Religion and the Homilies) of the Church of England, and of the Churches of the Anglican Communion which came from the mother Church, will surely find this to be true. The commitment to Scripture and Tradition is very obvious in the Books of Common Prayer, editions of which appeared in similar, but varying forms from 1549 until the 1962 (Canadian edition).

Since the 1960s, with the absorption of the new theologies and moralities, various changes have occurred in Anglicanism. Thus, there have appeared alternative ways alongside and often intertwined with the traditional Anglican Way. Nowhere is this more obvious than in the replacement of the classic *Books of Common Prayer,* which were in use around the world, with new *Books of Alternative Services* (books sometimes, as with the new American Episcopal Prayer Book, regrettably also called *The Book of Common Prayer*). We shall turn to the theological background to these new books in chapter ten below.

The Anglican Way - as it was

The theological basis of the English Reformation, and of the Reformed Catholicism which emerged, is most conveniently explained in terms of its commitment to *one Bible, two Testaments, three Creeds, four Councils and five Centuries*. This was the simple yet profound approach and explanation taken by the most prominent early apologists of the reformed Church of England - e.g., John Jewel, Richard Hooker, and Lancelot Andrewes. It shows that they had the same basic understanding of the meaning of "Protestant" as that set forth in Germany at the Diet of Speyer in 1529. At that time (if not so later!) "a Protestant" was a person who protested on behalf of the authority of the Bible, as that Bible was received and interpreted in the early undivided Church of the first five centuries.

One Bible. For most Protestants today there is no difference between two equations. The first is One Bible = Two Testaments and the second is Two Testaments = One Bible. Logically there is perhaps no difference; yet for the Reformers (following the patristic and medieval Church) the first equation is the right one. This is because to begin with the concept of the unity of the Bible affects the way we approach and view the contents of the whole Bible.

To speak of one Bible is to speak of one and the same God to whom both Testaments witness. The Lord God whom Moses met at the burning bush and who inspired the prophets of Israel to proclaim the word of the Lord is the same living God manifested in the life and ministry of Jesus of Nazareth. It is also to speak both of one self-revelation by this Lord God and one salvation which he provides. Of course there is a historical development in the way the revealing and saving God is known and encountered in space and time, but the essential point is that the unity of the revelation and salvation (based in the very unity of God himself) underlies the differences in historical manifestation.

The reformers of the sixteenth century insisted on the authority of the whole Bible in the Church. Article VI of the Church of England reads:

> Holy Scripture containeth all things necessary to salvation: so that whatsoever is not read therein, nor may be proved thereby, is not to be required of any man, that it should be believed as an article of the Faith, or be thought requisite or necessary to salvation. In the name of holy Scripture we do understand those Canonical Books of the Old and New Testament, of whose authority was never any doubt in the Church.

Then in the official *Book of Homilies* there is a powerful sermon on this theme, "On the reverend estimation of God's Word." Further, the prayerful approach to the whole Bible is well caught by the Collect for the Second Sunday in Advent:

> Blessed Lord, who has caused all holy Scriptures to be written for our learning; Grant that we may in such wise hear them, read, mark, learn, and inwardly digest them, that by patience and comfort of thy holy Word, we may embrace and ever hold fast the blessed hope of everlasting life, which thou hast given us in our Savior Jesus Christ.

Of course the reformers did not believe that all the books of the Bible are strictly equal in terms of their value for the Church. Naturally they gave pride of place to the books of the New Testament (and to the Gospels in particular) in terms of the daily readings in the Lectionary for the whole year.

Two Testaments. The Bible of the early Church was what we now call the Old Testament, and to this was added over a period of time those writings which we now call the New Testament. In other words, the one canon was expanded to include the writings of the apostles and evangelists. The new Collection certainly had two parts, but it was one Collection. So it was said of it that the essential message of the New Testament is concealed in the Old Testament, and thus the basic purpose and forward movement of the Old Testament is revealed or made clear by the New Testament. Thus a key way to read and interpret the Old Testament is through the use of typology. In the OT are the types and in the NT are the anti-types. Thus, Jesus as the Lamb of God is the anti-type, and the lambs of the sacrificial offerings of the Temple are the type. Article VII says this of the Old Testament:

> The Old Testament is not contrary to the New: for both in the Old and New Testament everlasting life is offered to Mankind by Christ, who is the only Mediator between God and Man, being both God and Man. Wherefore they are not to be heard, which feign that the old Fathers did look only for transitory promises. Although the Law given from God by Moses, as touching Ceremonies and Rites, do not bind Christian men, nor the civil precepts thereof ought of necessity to be received in any commonwealth; yet notwithstanding, no Christian man whatsoever is free from obedience of the Commandments which are called moral.

Here the "old Fathers" are the patriarchs of the Old Testament to whom it is stated God gave promises unto everlasting life. Further, the moral content of the revelation from God (in contrast to that revelation which was solely for Israel as a theocratic nation with a limited life-span) in the Old Testament is seen as binding for all time. Thus, Christians have traditionally been taught the Ten Commandments which are inscribed on the walls of many Anglican churches. Finally (and the article does not say this), from the "Ceremonies and Rites" have been taken types, pointing to Jesus Christ and the new covenant, inaugurated by his precious blood.

In contrast today, because of the specialization and the division of theology into disciplines in the university and seminary, there is professional study of the Old and the New Testaments. However, there is rarely any study in the modern theological curriculum which presumes and sets forth the unity of the Holy Scriptures and interprets the Old by means of typology. This is nearly as true of evangelical as of liberal seminaries. The logic and practice everywhere followed seems to be that of Two Testaments = One Bible, with little emphasis on the unity.

Three Creeds. The Bible as Holy Scripture never existed apart from the Church of God in space and time. So it is appropriate to speak of the Bible as an authoritative Collection (made by the early Church) of authoritative books (the author of each inspired by the Holy Spirit). The Church which made the collection of books had a doctrinal basis. This is found in its clearest form in its Creeds, which are summaries of basic biblical themes and teaching. They were used for baptism and for stating what is believed, taught and confessed by the Church.

The creed known as the Apostles' Creed was used as the basis for the confession of faith in holy baptism. Thus, it is simple and easily committed to memory. That which is known as the Nicene Creed was produced by the bishops of the Church at the Council of Nicea in AD 325 and then fine-tuned at the next Council in Constantinople in 381. This creed began (325) as a statement of what the Church holds to be the truth concerning the relation of Jesus Christ to the Father and then developed (381) into a statement of God as the Holy Trinity. It became the profession of faith said by all believers in the Eucharist of the Sunday worship of the churches.

The third Creed was only used in the West from the fifth century and is known either as the Athanasian Creed or as the "Quicunque Vult" (the first words in the original Latin). This is longer than the other two and gives a precise statement of the doctrines of the Holy Trinity and of the Person of Jesus Christ. In the Church of England it was appointed to be used on Trinity Sunday and on other specific days. Some parts of the Anglican Communion have dropped the use of the Athanasian Creed, and it is not found in their Prayer Books. This is so of the American Episcopal Church from its 1789 Book (though it is printed as a historical document in the 1979 Book).

Four Councils. A basic claim of the reformers was that they wanted to reclaim and recover the Faith of the early, undivided Church of the first five centuries or so - before the division between East and West and before the beginning of the "Dark Ages." So they laid great emphasis upon the teaching officially sent forth from the first four Councils - Nicea (325), Constantinople (381), Ephesus (431) and Chalcedon (451). From these Councils they learned the fundamental doctrines which answered the questions; Who is God?, Who is Jesus?, and What is the Gospel? However, as they insisted, they only received these doctrines because it was obvious to them that they were truly faithful to the teaching of Holy Scripture. Further, they fully recognized that such councils could err and in fact later medieval councils had erred.

It is sometimes asked why they did not opt for seven councils for there were (by common agreement today) seven truly ecumenical councils in which East and West were involved. The answer is that they knew little or nothing about the seventh (Nicea II, 787) and judged the other two (Constantinople II, 553; Constantinople III, 680-681) only to have fine-tuned the Christology set forth in the Definition of the Faith by the Council of Chalcedon in 451.

Five Centuries. This affirmation goes with that of the Four Councils. It was a recognition that the reformed Church of England would follow the general lines of development of theology, liturgy and polity of these five centuries. Thus the recognition of Sunday as the Lord's Day, as the day of worship; the use of the Church Year from Advent through Christmas and Easter to Pentecost / Trinity season; the reading of the Bible through a structured Lectionary; liturgical worship rather than free worship; the celebration of the Holy Communion on Sundays and holy days, with daily prayer in the morning and evening of every day in the church; and the retention of the three-fold ministry of bishop, presbyter and deacon.

In terms of liturgy, Cranmer looked to the Rites of which he had knowledge from the Early Church (e.g., the Liturgy of St Chrysostom) before he produced the 1549 *Book of Com-*

mon Prayer. In the seventeenth century, the study of the liturgical texts of the Eastern Church was taken very seriously by the Caroline divines. This work was continued by those (9 bishops, 400 priests with laity) whom we call the Nonjurors, who were forced to leave the Church of England during the reign of William and Mary from 1688, because they could not in conscience take the Oath of Allegiance to them (having already made it to James II and his successors). And this work was continued by bishops and theologians of the Scottish Episcopal Church.

Bishop Dowden, in his book on the Scottish Prayer Book has this to say about patristic sources and the Eucharistic Prayer in the Order for Holy Communion:

> The liturgiologists belonging to the school of theologians from which our Communion Office has proceeded were satisfied of the apostolic origin of the Invocation [the prayer for the descent of the Spirit on the elements]; and they would certainly be entirely justified in claiming for it high antiquity. They knew that it existed in the four patriarchates of Christendom - Alexandria, Antioch, Jerusalem, and Constantinople...They looked to the Greek liturgies, though disfigured by many later additions, as retaining the structure and essence of the Eucharistic worship of Christ's Church in its purest age. There was one feature which they found prevailing in the Greek liturgies, viz. the arrangement of the parts of the great Prayer of Consecration in the order - (1) Recital of the narrative of the Institution, (2) the Oblation of the Elements, (3) the Prayer to God the Father for the descent of the Holy Spirit, that he might make the Elements the Body and Blood of Christ; and this they regarded as of such high moment that a return to it in their own forms of worship seemed to them a manifest duty. (*The Scottish Communion Office 1764*, p.9.)

The particular liturgies that they examined included the Liturgy of St James, the Liturgy of St Basil, the Liturgy of St Chrysostom, the Liturgy of St Mark, and the Liturgy of St Clement.

Reflections

The doctrine within and arising from this basis and method became both the *lex credendi*, "the law of believing," and the *lex orandi*, "the law of praying," of the Church of England. It is found within the *Book of Common Prayer* (first edition in 1549; revised editions 1552; 1559; 1604; 1662), which provided the services for the public worship on weekdays and the Lord's Day, as well as the occasional offices (e.g., baptism, marriage and the burial of the dead) of the Church. In other words, the teaching set forth in the Creeds and Articles of Religion from Scripture and Tradition was understood to be the basis for the form of words of the Daily Offices, of the Administration of the Lord's Supper and of all the other services.

Further, an integral part of the *Book of Common Prayer* is the Catechism, which is an exposition of the Creed, the Ten Commandments and the Lord's Prayer. Then, of course, a Lectionary is an indispensable part of this whole Liturgy; and where this is followed, then the whole Bible is read through systematically each year in a doctrinal way; and the Psalter, the prayer-book of the Lord Jesus, is prayed once a month.

It has been claimed, with some justification, that the Church of England (and therefore, the Anglican Communion of Churches developing from it) is not a confessional Church like the Reformed and Lutheran (who have their carefully constructed Confessions of Faith). That is, the *Thirty-Nine Articles* are more as a signpost through the muddy waters of the sixteenth century than a full-blown Confession of Faith. What is certainly true is that Anglicanism, with or without a Confession of Faith and true to itself, proclaims and contains the *lex credendi* in the form of the *lex orandi* of the Church.

When *The Book of Common Prayer* was revised from the 1662 model in terms of anything other than local adaption (e.g., prayers for the local nation instead of the monarch in England), then the appeal was made to Scripture or Tradition or both. This is especially true, as we have already noted above and shall abundantly see in this book, in terms of the actual arrangement of and the precise contents of the Service of Holy Communion. Changes began to be made in the Eucharist in the seventeenth century (e.g., in the Scottish Episcopal Church) on the basis of an appeal to the Church of "the Fathers" of the third to the fifth centuries.

Obviously, the exposition and teaching of this Faith, which is the Anglican Way, was not identical in all the parishes of England; and neither was it uniform in books explaining the Anglican Way. The Church of England (unlike some parts of the Anglican Communion of Churches) has always had a spectrum of interpretation of doctrine which goes from very Protestant to very Catholic. Further, it has contained schools of thought or churchmanship ranging from high to low in terms of the use of ceremonial and the frequency of the celebration of the sacrament of Holy Communion. However, what can be clearly said of all theologies genuinely arising from the doctrines of the *Book of Common Prayer* and the Articles of Religion is that they are classically Catholic and Trinitarian in their teaching concerning the Father, the Son and the Holy Spirit, God; and they are classically Protestant (or Augustinian) in their teaching that salvation is by the grace of God through faith.

It may be claimed that as long as the traditional Prayer Book was the basis for worship in England or wherever else the Anglican Way had been planted, it was always obvious to the alert worshipper whether or not the parish priest in his teaching and preaching was straying into other views of God, of Christ, of salvation and of sin than are provided within the Book. Having said all this, I must freely admit that sound, orthodox doctrine - as is found in the successive editions of the *Book of Common Prayer* - lives best in lively, God-fearing hearts and in the devout worship of faithful congregations. No Prayer Book, however good in content, and however prominent in the pews, can preserve godliness and orthodoxy in and of itself.

CHAPTER THREE

Reformed Catholic:
the 1549 BCP

The first *Book of Common Prayer* was published for the Church of England in 1549, and it was primarily the work of Thomas Cranmer, Archbishop of Canterbury. Since the Church had existed in England for centuries, it was not the first book of prayers and orders of worship for the English Church. What existed before it were the traditional Latin books which were intended primarily for clergy. They came with such titles as the Missal, the Breviary, the Manual, the Pontifical, and the Processional. Also several books in English had appeared in the 1540s to encourage lay devotion and participation. Of these the most important was *The Order of the Communion* (1548).

The new *Book of Common Prayer*, however, broke new ground and established a totally new pattern. It was the first service book in English intended for all clergy and for all laity throughout the kingdom and containing the chief services of the Church. Henceforth, all local or diocesan forms of service were to cease; they had been superseded by this book.

As long as you had the Bible, it was possible with the new *Book of Common Prayer* either to conduct or participate fully in all public worship or occasional offices. You needed no other book but these two. Matins and Evensong, the Order for Holy Communion, the occasional offices of baptism, confirmation, marriage, burial and the purification of women after childbirth, as well as for the Visitation of the Sick were all there - along with the Introits, Collects, Epistles and Gospels for Sundays and Holy Days and a Lectionary for the whole year. In 1550 a musical edition of the parts of the *BCP* normally sung in churches was printed; the musical setting was by John Marbeck, a minor canon at Windsor Castle.

The Book of Common Prayer contained what may be best called a Reformed Catholicism, an English form of western Christian worship. Thus, there was both continuity and discontinuity with the medieval Church, its theology, spirituality and its forms of worship. Looking back over the centuries from a bird's high view, the discontinuities are obvious - e.g., the absence of the elevation of the Host (the highpoint of the Mass for the non-communicating participant of the medieval Mass); English not Latin; minimum rather than maximum ceremonial; Communion in two kinds not one; two daily services (Matins and Evensong) rather than five (Matins, Lauds, Prime, Vespers, and Compline); a simpler and shorter form of the burial service, and a new form of the doctrine of God's grace (the Lutheran doctrine of justification by faith).

Also obvious are the continuities - the identical Creeds (Apostles', Nicene, Athanasian); the addressing of the Father through the Son and by the Holy Spirit in worship; the centrality of the Psalter as the primary book of prayers for daily use; the use of the same church buildings with the same bishops, priests and deacons as ministers of Word and Sacrament; and the continuance of the occasional offices of baptism, marriage, burial and the churching of women after childbirth in the local parish church.

Though much happened in the reign of Henry VIII in terms of weakening the traditional Catholicism, the real break came soon after Edward VI became king in 1546. Eamon Duffy writes:

> Tudor men and women had stoically endured many religious changes in the reign of Henry. They had seen the monasteries and friaries go, the shrines pillaged, the lights in the parish churches snuffed out, the Pope's name

scratched or cut out of the parish liturgical books and their own primers, the abolition of many of the traditional feast-days. There had been Protestant preaching, even, in some places, image-breaking and burning. But these early Edwardine changes were recognized as something new, something different. The Marian church-wardens of Stanford in the Vale in Berkshire, stock-taking after six years of destruction, articulated a very generally shared perception when they dated "the time of schism when this Realm was divided from the Catholic Church" not from the early 1530s but from the "second year of Edward VI," when "all godly ceremonies and good uses were taken out of the Church within this realm (*The Stripping of the Altars*, 1992, p.462).

The intense effort to remove all traces of medieval super-stition, ceremonial and devotions began before the publication of the 1549 *BCP* - whose "Mass" contained no elevation of the Host.

The Supper of the Lord

Our interest here is with "The Supper of the Lord and the Holy Communion, commonly called the Mass." We may note that "The Supper of the Lord" is the name taken from Hermann von Wied's service of the same name, printed in Cologne in 1544. "Holy Communion" is a vernacular name, applied to the whole service for the first time, and "Mass" is the traditional medieval name as well as the Lutheran name in use in Germany.

The order of the service is set out below:

The Lord's Prayer
The Collect for Purity
Kyrie Eleison
Gloria in excelsis
The Salutation
The Collect of the Day
The Collect for the King
The Epistle
The Gospel
The Nicene Creed
The Sermon or Homily

An Exhortation, II or III
The Offertory
Sursum corda
The Canon - Prayer for the Church
    Consecration
    Oblation
The Lord's Prayer
The Peace
"Christ our paschal Lamb..."
"Ye that do truly repent ye"
The Confession of sins
The Absolution
The Comfortable Words of Scripture
"We do not presume..."
Priest and people receive Communion
Agnus Dei (sung during Communion)
The post-Communion sentences
The prayer of thanksgiving
The Blessing

If this order is compared with the Sarum Rite, the well known form of the Roman Rite used in England, a relation can be seen at various points. One of these is that the *Canon* (the Eucharistic Prayer) has three parts to it. While the contents of the three parts have certain similarities, the influence of Protestant thought and sources is obvious in the mind and pen of Archbishop Cranmer in the 1549 text.

The Setting of the Eucharistic Prayer

Then shall the Minister take so much bread and wine, as shall suffice for the persons appointed to receive the holy communion, laying the bread upon the corporas, or else in the paten, or in some other comely thing prepared for that purpose: and putting the wine into the chalice, or else in some fair or convenient cup prepared for that use (if the chalice will not serve) putting thereto a little pure and clean water, and setting both the bread and wine upon the altar. Then the Priest shall say,

               The Lord be with you.
Answer: **And with thy spirit.**

Priest: **Lift up your hearts.**
Answer: **We lift them up unto the Lord.**
Priest: **Let us give thanks to our Lord God.**
Answer: **It is meet and right so to do.**
The Priest: **It is very meet, right, and our bounden duty that we should at all times and in all places give thanks to thee, O Lord, holy Father, almighty everlasting God.**

Here shall follow the proper preface, according to the time (if there be any specially appointed), or else immediately shall follow,

Therefore with angels, etc.

Proper Prefaces

Upon Christmas Day
Because thou didst give Jesus Christ, thine only Son, to be born as this day for us; who, by the operation of the Holy Ghost, was made very man of the substance of the Virgin Mary his mother; and that without spot of sin, to make us clean from all sin. Therefore, etc.

Upon Easter Day
But chiefly are we bound to praise thee for the glorious resurrection of thy Son Jesus Christ our Lord: for he is the very Paschal Lamb, which was offered for us, and hath taken away the sin of the world; who by his death hath destroyed death, and by his rising to life again hath restored to us everlasting life. Therefore, etc.

Upon the Ascension Day
Through thy most dear beloved Son, Jesus Christ our Lord; who, after his most glorious resurrection, manifestly appeared to all his disciples, and in their sight ascended up into heaven to prepare a place for us; that where he is, thither might we also ascend, and reign with him in glory. Therefore, etc.

Upon Whit Sunday

Through Jesus Christ our Lord; according to whose most true promise the Holy Ghost came down this day from heaven with a sudden great sound, as it had been a mighty wind, in the likeness of fiery tongues, lighting upon the apostles, to teach them, and to lead them to all truth, giving them both the gift of divers languages, and also boldness with fervent zeal, constantly to preach the gospel unto all nations; whereby we are brought out of darkness and error, into the clear light and true knowledge of thee, and of thy Son Jesus Christ. Therefore, etc.

Upon the feast of the Trinity

It is very meet, right, and our bounden duty, that we should at all times and in all places, give thanks to thee, O Lord, Almighty, everlasting God, which art one God, one Lord; not one only Person, but three Persons in one substance. For that which we believe of the glory of the Father, the same we believe of the Son, and of the Holy Ghost, without any difference or inequality. Whom with angels, etc.

After which Preface shall follow immediately,

Therefore with angels and archangels, and with all the holy company of heaven, we laud and magnify thy glorious name; evermore praising thee, and saying,

Holy, holy, holy, Lord God of hosts: heaven and earth are full of thy glory. Hosannah in the highest. Blessed is he that cometh in the name of the Lord. Glory to thee, O Lord, in the highest.

This the Clerks shall also sing.
When the Clerks have done singing, then shall the Priest or Deacon turn him to the people, and say,

Let us pray for the whole state of Christ's Church.

Then the priest, turning him to the altar, shall say or sing, plainly and distinctly, this prayer following:

Almighty and everliving God, which by thy holy apostle hast taught us to make prayers, and supplications, and to give thanks for all men; We humbly beseech thee most mercifully to receive these our prayers, which we offer unto thy divine Majesty; beseeching thee to inspire continually the universal church with the spirit of truth, unity, and concord: and grant, that all they that do confess thy holy name may agree in the truth of thy holy word, and live in unity and godly love. Specially we beseech thee to save and defend thy servant Edward our King; that under him we may be godly and quietly governed; and grant unto his whole council, and to all that be put in authority under him, that they may truly and indifferently minister justice, to the punishment of wickedness and vice, and to the maintenance of God's true religion and virtue. Give grace (O heavenly Father) to all bishops, pastors and curates that they may both by their life and doctrine set forth thy true and lively word, and rightly and duly administer thy holy sacraments. And to all thy people give thy heavenly grace; that with meek heart and due reverence, they may hear and receive thy holy word; truly serving thee in holiness and righteousness all the days of their life. And we most humbly beseech thee of thy goodness (O Lord) to comfort and succour all them, which in this transitory life be in trouble, sorrow, need, sickness, or any other adversity. And especially we commend unto thy merciful goodness this congregation, which is here assembled in thy name, to celebrate the commemoration of the most glorious death of thy Son. And here we do give unto thee most high praise, and hearty thanks, for the wonderful grace and virtue declared in thy saints, from the beginning of the world; and chiefly in the glorious and most blessed Virgin Mary, mother of thy Son Jesu Christ our Lord and God; and in the holy patriarchs, prophets, apostles and martyrs, whose examples (O Lord) and stedfastness in thy faith, and keeping thy holy commandments, grant us to follow. We commend unto thy mercy (O Lord) all other thy servants, which are departed hence from us, with the sign of faith, and now do rest in the sleep of peace: grant unto them, we beseech thee, thy mercy, and everlasting peace; and that, at the day of the general resurrection, we and all they which be of the mystical body of thy Son, may altogether be set on his right hand, and hear that his most joyful voice: Come unto me, O ye that be blessed of my Father, and possess the kingdom, which is prepared for you from the beginning of the world. Grant this, O Father, for Jesus Christ's sake, our only Mediator and Advocate.

O God, heavenly Father, which of thy tender mercy didst give thine only Son Jesu Christ to suffer death upon the cross for our redemption; who made there (by his one oblation once offered) a full, perfect, and sufficient sacrifice, oblation, and satisfaction, for the sins of the whole world; and did institute, and in his holy gospel command us to celebrate a perpetual memory of that his precious death, until his coming again: hear us (O merciful Father) we beseech thee; and with thy Holy Spirit and word vouchsafe to bless [*the sign of the cross*] and sanctify [*the sign of the cross*] these thy gifts and creatures of bread and wine, that they may be unto us the body and blood of thy most dearly beloved Son Jesus Christ, who, in the same night that he was betrayed, took bread, [*the bread is taken into his hands*] and when he had blessed, and given thinks, he brake it, and gave it to his disciples, saying, Take, eat; this is my body which is given for you; do this in remembrance of me.

Likewise after supper he took the cup, [*the cup is taken in his hands*] and when he had given thanks, he gave it to them, saying, Drink ye all of this; for this is my blood of the new Testament, which is shed for you and for many for remission of sins. Do this, as oft as you shall drink it, in remembrance of me.

These words before rehearsed are to be said, turning still to the altar, without any elevation or shewing the Sacrament to the people.

Wherefore, O Lord and heavenly Father, according to the institution of thy dearly beloved Son our Saviour Jesu Christ, we thy humble servants do celebrate and make here before thy divine Majesty, with these thy holy gifts, the memorial which thy Son hath willed us to make; having in remembrance his blessed passion, mighty resurrection, and glorious ascension; rendering unto thee most hearty thanks for the innumerable benefits procured unto us by the same; entirely desiring thy fatherly goodness mercifully to accept this our sacrifice of praise and thanksgiving; most humbly beseeching thee to grant, that by the merits and death of thy Son Jesus Christ and through faith in his blood, we and all thy whole church may obtain remission of our sins, and all other benefits of his passion. And here we offer and present unto thee (O Lord) ourselves, our souls and bodies, to be a reasonable, holy and lively sacrifice unto thee; humbly beseeching thee, that whosoever shall be partakers of this holy communion may worthily receive the most precious body and blood of thy Son, Jesus Christ, and be fulfilled with thy grace and heavenly benediction, and made one body with thy Son Jesu Christ, that he may dwell in them, and they in him. And although we be unworthy (through our manifold sins) to offer unto thee any sacrifice, yet we beseech thee to accept this our bounden duty and service, and command these our prayers and supplications, by the ministry of thy holy angels, to be brought up into thy holy tabernacle, before the sight of thy divine Majesty; not weighing our merits, but pardoning our offences, through Christ our Lord; by whom, and with whom, in the unity of the Holy Ghost, all honour and glory be unto thee, O Father Almighty, world without end. Amen.

Let us pray.

As our Saviour Christ hath commanded and taught us, we are bold to say, Our Father, which art in heaven, hallowed be thy name. Thy kingdom come. Thy will be done in earth, as it is in heaven. Give us this day our daily bread. And forgive us our trespasses, as we forgive them that trespass against us. And lead us not into temptation.

The Answer. But deliver us from evil.

Then shall the Priest say,

The peace of the Lord be always with you.

The Clerks: And with thy spirit.

The Priest: Christ our Paschal Lamb is offered up for us, once for all, when he bare our sins on his body upon the cross; for he is the very Lamb of God that taketh away the sins of the world: therefore let us keep a joyful and holy feast with the Lord.

Here the Priest shall turn him toward those that come to the holy Communion, and shall say,

You that do truly and earnestly repent you of your sins to Almighty God, and be in love and charity with your neighbours, and intend to lead a new life, following the commandments of God, and walking from henceforth in his holy ways; Draw near, and take this holy sacrament to your comfort; make your humble confession to Almighty God, and to his holy church here gathered together in his name, meekly kneeling upon your knees.

Then shall this general confession be made, in the name of all those that are minded to receive the holy Communion, either by one of them, or else by one of the Ministers, or by the Priest himself, all kneeling humbly upon their knees.

Almighty God, Father of our Lord Jesus Christ, Maker of all things, judge of all men; we acknowledge and bewail our manifold sins and wickedness, which we, from time to time, most grievously have committed, by thought, word, and deed, against thy divine Majesty, provoking most justly thy wrath and indignation against us. We do earnestly repent, and be heartily sorry for these our misdoings; the remembrance of them is grievous unto us; the burden of them is intolerable. Have mercy upon us, have mercy upon us, most merciful Father; for thy Son our Lord Jesus Christ's sake, forgive us all that is past; and grant that we may ever hereafter serve and please thee in newness of life, to the honour and glory of thy name; through Jesus Christ our Lord.

Then shall the Priest stand up, and turning himself to the people, say thus:

Almighty God, our heavenly Father, who of his great mercy hath promised forgiveness of sins to all them which with hearty repentance and true faith turn unto him; Have mercy upon you; pardon and deliver you from all your sins; confirm and strengthen you in all goodness; and bring you to everlasting life; through Jesus Christ our Lord. Amen.

Then shall the Priest also say.

Hear what comfortable words our Saviour Christ saith to all that truly turn to him.

Come unto me all that travail, and be heavy laden, and I shall refresh you. So God loved the world, that he gave his only-begotten Son, to the end that all that believe in him should not perish, but have life everlasting.

Hear also what Saint Paul saith.

This is a true saying, and worthy of all men to be received. that Jesus Christ came into this world to save sinners.

Hear also what Saint John saith.

If any man sin, we have an Advocate with the Father, Jesus Christ the righteous; and he is the propitiation for our sins.

Then shall the Priest, turning him to God's board, kneel down, and say in the name of all that receive the communion, this prayer following:

We do not presume to come to this thy table (O merciful Lord) trusting in our own righteousness, but in thy manifold and great mercies. We be not worthy so much as to gather up the crumbs under thy table; but thou art the same Lord whose property is always to have mercy: Grant us therefore (gracious Lord) so to eat the flesh of thy dear Son Jesus Christ, and to drink his blood in these holy Mysteries, that we may continually dwell in him and he in us, that our sinful bodies may be made clean by his body and our souls washed through his most precious blood. Amen.

Then shall the Priest first receive the Communion in both kinds himself, and next deliver it to other Ministers, if there be any present, (that they may be ready to help the chief Minister) and after to the people.

And when he delivereth the Sacrament of the body of Christ, he shall say to every one these words:

The body of our Lord Jesus Christ which was given for thee, preserve thy body and soul unto everlasting life.

And the Minister delivering the Sacrament of the blood, and giving every one to drink once and no more, shall say,

The blood of our Lord Jesus Christ which was shed for thee, preserve thy body and soul unto everlasting life.

If there be a Deacon or other Priest, then shall he follow with the Chalice; and as the priest ministereth the Sacrament of the body, so shall he (for more expedition) minister the Sacrament of the blood, in form before written.

In the communion time the Clerks shall sing,

O Lamb of God, that takest away the sins of the world: have mercy upon us. (twice)
O Lamb of God, that takest away the sins of the world: grant us thy peace.

Beginning so soon as the Priest doth receive the holy Communion, and when the Communion is ended, then shall the Clerks sing the post-Communion.

(Then follows a selection of twenty-two Scripture verses to be sung)

Then the Priest shall give thanks to God, in the name of all them that have communicated, turning him first to the people and saying,

	The Lord be with you
The Answer:	**And with thy spirit.**
The Priest:	**Let us pray.**

Almighty and everliving God, we most heartily thank thee, for that thou hast vouchsafed to feed us in these holy Mysteries, with the spiritual food of the most precious body and blood of thy Son our Saviour Jesus Christ, and hast assured us (duly receiving the same) of thy favour and goodness towards us, and that we be very members incorporate in thy mystical body, which is the blessed company of all faithful people, and heirs through hope of thy everlasting kingdom, by the merits of the most precious death and passion of thy dear Son. We therefore most humbly beseech thee, O heavenly Father, so to assist us with thy grace, that we may continue in that holy fellowship, and do all such good works, as thou hast prepared for us to walk in: through Jesus Christ our Lord, to whom, with thee and the Holy Ghost, be all honour and glory, world without end. *Amen.*

Comment

It will be noticed that in the initial rubrics it is assumed that the traditional Mixed Chalice will be retained. The mixing of water with wine symbolized the water and blood which flowed from the Saviour's side (John 19:34). However, no Lavabo, or washing of the hands is required, even though this was the medieval custom and justified or authorized by Psalm 26:6, "I will wash my hands in innocency, O Lord; and so will I go to thine altar."

In the first section, there is prayer for the universal church, for the king, his council and the nation, and then for the clergy and people, especially those in need. These petitions are followed by thanksgiving for the grace of God revealed in his saints of both the Old and New Testaments, chiefly the Blessed Virgin Mary.

In the medieval Sarum Rite, after the listing of the BVM, the apostles and martyrs, are the words: "by whose merits and prayers grant thou that in all things we may be defended with the help of thy protection..." Later, the same Rite has these words: "by the intercession of the blessed, glorious, and ever-virgin Mary, the mother of God, and thy blessed apostles, Peter and Paul; and Andrew, with all saints, give peace in our days..." In contrast, in the 1549 BCP it is the example rather than the intercession of the saints which is particularly noted. Obviously, Cranmer was seeking to correct what were deemed to be abuses in "prayers to the saints."

Commemoration of the saints is followed by prayer for the dead, who have had Christian burial and who rest in the sleep of peace. It is asked of the Lord that they shall partake in the resurrection of the righteous and be placed at the right hand of the Son of man at the Last Judgment. The Sarum Rite beseeches the Lord that to "all such as rest in Christ" he will grant "a place of refreshing, of light, and of peace."

Turning to the second section we find several notable features. First, there is the very clear statement concerning the death of Jesus Christ at Calvary. Here the voice of the

Protestant Reformation speaks loudly! No one could think that this new Mass included in any way whatsoever a repeat of, or a re-enactment of, the perfect sacrifice of Calvary.

The *epiclesis* or invocation of the Holy Spirit to bless the gifts of bread and wine is a feature taken by Cranmer from the early liturgies of the Church in the patristic period. There is no parallel to this in the Sarum Rite or the Western Rite. In contrast, the Eastern Liturgies have an explicit *epiclesis* and probably Cranmer had looked to what we call Eastern Orthodoxy for this feature.

The Words of Institution, which close the second section, represent a harmonization from both the accounts of the Last Supper in the Gospels and from Paul's words in 1 Corinthians 11. The rubrics which require the sign of the cross at the *epiclesis* or invocation, make no allowance for the elevation of the "bread" and "the chalice" as in the Sarum Rite.

The third section begins with the memorial, *anamnesis* or commemoration of "the blessed passion, mighty resurrection, and glorious ascension" [note the adjectives] of Jesus Christ and continues with the offering of a sacrifice of thanksgiving for the same. While there is no offering of the already consecrated bread and wine (as in the Sarum Rite), there is the self-offering of the worshippers and the request that all shall be worthy partakers of the most precious body and blood of Christ.

Finally, the ministry of angels (plural) is seen in this Reformed Catholic prayer as bringing the prayers of the worshippers to the throne of God. In contrast, in the Sarum Rite the holy angel (singular) is seen as taking the gifts from the altar on earth to the altar in the presence of the divine majesty.

There has been much speculation concerning the precise doctrine of the presence of Christ in the Sacrament intended by the 1549 text. It seems to be the case that as the Archbishop of Canterbury, with concern for the unity of the nation and Church, Cranmer put together a Canon which was open to a variety of interpretations.

Transubstantiation (the whole bread becomes the whole Body and the whole wine becomes the whole Blood) is rejected. However, there is plenty of space for a belief in the Presence of Christ in or with the elements. Certainly the words of administration suggest the real presence: "The Body of our Lord Jesus Christ..." and "The Blood of our Lord Jesus Christ...," as also do the words of the final prayer: "...with the spiritual food of the most precious body and blood of thy Son." Further, it was required that communicants receive the consecrated bread directly upon their tongues, rather than in their hands. Finally, the whole service and especially the Canon do convey a profound sense of sacramental Mystery.

Though the 1549 *BCP* did not have long enough use in England to win the hearts and minds of English worshippers, it was never forgotten. It was always there to be used either for inspiration in the reform of later Prayer Books or for actual use (in recent times) in parts of the Anglican Communion of Churches (e.g., in the West Indies). It is not, I think, a Rite for regular public worship today; rather, it is a Rite to inspire us today in recognizing the Reformed Catholic nature of Anglicanism and its dependence not only on Western Catholicism but also upon the early Eastern (patristic) Church.

CHAPTER FOUR

Anglican Protestant: the 1552 BCP

Whenever there is the rejection or loss of a time honored tradition, institution or activity by a people, there will always be many suggestions as to its replacement in the present and for the future. Such was the case in England after the rejection of the Latin Mass, which had been at the center of religious life for a millennium. In this situation the 1549 *BCP* was Cranmer's attempt to take the best of the past from West and East and to marry it to the important biblical, theological and social insights of the Protestant Reformation, and thereby provide for the corporate worship of Almighty God in England. However, the new Prayer Book was received by a Church and nation which were in ferment. Some wanted to return to the old medieval ways; some wished for minimal revision of the old ways; some believed that a moderate revision was most appropriate; others wanted major revisions of the old ways.

Cranmer, with his pastoral concern as Archbishop of Canterbury, stood in the middle of the ferment. His 1549 *BCP* pleased neither the old Catholics nor the new Protestants. Further, those royal advisors who had the ear of the young king, Edward VI, wanted to see a cleaner break with the medieval past. What was happening in Protestant Switzerland and Germany, together with the arguments of major Protestant theologians such as Martin Bucer and John

Hooper, carried much weight. So within three years of the publication of the first *Book of Common Prayer,* there appeared another book of the same name but with changed content.

One characteristic of Cranmer was his deep sense of his duty to obey his king. Thus, he with others, made the changes in the text of the 1549 *BCP* which the monarch (as advised by his council) required, but he probably hated having to make any changes at all. What is clear is that he obeyed his earthly sovereign, who required the changes.

The Second Prayer Book became the only legal service book in England on November 1, 1552. Yet, like its predecessor its public life was very short. Edward VI died and Queen Mary succeeded to the throne on July 6, 1553. Soon the old Latin Mass legally replaced the English services. However, the 1552 *BCP* continued to be used but not in England. English exiles at friendly Protestant cities such as Frankfort and Geneva in Europe based their worship upon it.

A Comparison

When a comparison is made of the 1549 and 1552 Books, the first impression of a modern reader is that they are very similar. More careful study reveals that the 1552 enjoins more congregational participation in worship than the 1549. Further, old names are dropped (e.g. Matins and Evensong) and replaced by new ones (Morning and Evening Prayer). Then, to the newly named Morning and Evening Prayer are added a penitential introduction, including a Confession and Absolution. There are also significant changes of structure and content in the services of Public Baptism, Burial and the Churching of Women.

In the service of the Holy Communion, which is our chief concern, there are three types of change. *First of all,* there is a change in structure. The Canon of three parts (Prayer for the Church, Consecration and Oblation) was broken up, and the parts placed apart from each other (see the Order below). This was done to make sure that there would be no adoration of Christ in the consecrated elements and that no doctrine of the Eucharist as a propitiatory sacrifice for the living and the dead could be read into the service. Also the *Gloria in excelsis* was moved to the end of the service, and at the beginning of the service the Ten Commandments were inserted.

In the second place, there are changes in language. The Prayer for the Church lost its references to the saints and the departed and became prayer for "the Church militant here in earth." Further, new words for the administration of Holy Communion and the removal of the *Benedictus,* "Blessed is he...," from the *Sanctus* were intended to exclude any idea of transubstantiation or the corporeal presence of Christ.

Thirdly, there are changes in the instructions for the performance of this liturgy. Mass vestments are forbidden. A bishop is to wear a rochet, and the priest is to wear a surplice. The holy table is to covered by a white linen cloth and the celebrant is to kneel at the north side. There are to be no manual acts of holding the bread and wine during the Consecration. Further, at the distribution of the Communion, the consecrated bread is to be put into the hands not mouths of the communicants.

At the end of "The Order for the Administration of the Lord's Supper," there appears the "Black Rubric," which was a very late addition to the new *BCP,* by an Order of Council of October 27, 1552. This long rubric or explanatory comment was certainly not the composition of Cranmer. It may be traced to the general opposition of Continental Protestants to kneeling at Holy Communion, and in particular to Bishop Hooper. Here is the essential part of it:

> Whereas it is ordained in the Book of Common Prayer in the administration of the Lord's Supper, that the communicants kneeling should receive the Holy Communion: which thing being well meant, for a signification of the humble and grateful acknowledging of the benefits of Christ, given unto the worthy receiver, and to avoid the profanation and disorder, which about the Holy Communion might else ensue: lest yet the same kneeling might be

thought or taken otherwise, we do declare that it is not meant thereby, that any adoration is done, or ought to be done, either unto the sacramental bread or wine there bodily received, or to any real and essential presence there being of Christ's natural flesh and blood. For as concerning the sacramental bread and wine, they remain still in their very natural substances, and therefore may not be adored, for that were idolatry to be abhorred of all faithful Christians. And as concerning the natural body and blood of our Saviour Christ, they are in heaven and not here. For it is against the truth of Christ's true natural body to be in more places than in one at the one time.

So kneeling is a good thing, but the fact of it must not be taken to imply anything concerning the precise nature of the presence of Christ in or at the Sacrament.

The contents of the 1552 Order for Holy Communion are as follows:

The Lord's Prayer
The Collect for Purity
The Ten Commandments & the *Kyrie eleison*
The Collect of the Day
The Collect for the King
The Epistle
The Gospel
The Creed
The Sermon
The Offertory
The Prayer for the Church
Exhortation I or II & III
"Ye that do truly..."
The Confession of Sins
The Absolution
The Comfortable Words
The *Sursum Corda*
"We do not presume..."
Prayer of Consecration
The Distribution & Communion
The Lord's Prayer
The Prayer of Thanksgiving (Choice from Two)
The *Gloria in Excelsis*
The Blessing

This general order was to remain that of the English (in contrast to Scottish) Books of Common Prayer throughout the sixteenth and seventeenth centuries and into the modern era.

The Consecration Prayer and its Context

The text of the 1552 Rite from the *Sursum corda* through to the *Gloria in Excelsis* is as follows:

Priest: **Lift up your hearts.**
Answer: **We lift them up unto the Lord.**
Priest: **Let us give thanks unto our Lord God.**
Answer: **It is meet and right so to do.**
Priest: **It is very meet, right, and our bounden duty, that we should at all times, and in all places, give thanks unto thee, O Lord, holy Father, almighty, everlasting God.**

Here shall follow the proper Preface, according to the time, if there be any specially appointed:

After which Preface shall follow immediately,

Therefore with angels and archangels, and with all the company of heaven, we laud and magnify thy glorious name, evermore praising thee, and saying,

Holy, holy, holy, Lord God of hosts, heaven and earth are full of thy glory. Glory be to thee, O Lord most high.

Then shall the Priest, kneeling down at God's board, say, in the name of all them that shall receive the communion, this prayer following:

We do not presume to come to this thy table (O merciful Lord) trusting in our own righteousness, but in thy manifold and great mercies. We be not worthy so much as to gather up the crumbs under thy table; but thou art the same

Lord whose property is always to have mercy: Grant us therefore (gracious Lord) so to eat the flesh of thy dear Son Jesus Christ, and to drink his blood, that our sinful bodies may be made clean by his body, and our souls washed through his most precious blood, and that we may evermore dwell in him, and he in us. Amen.

Then the Priest, standing up, shall say as followeth:

Almighty God, our heavenly Father, which of thy tender mercy didst give thine only Son Jesus Christ to suffer death upon the cross for our redemption; who made there (by his one oblation of himself once offered) a full, perfect, and sufficient sacrifice, oblation, and satisfaction for the sins of the whole world; and did institute, and in his holy Gospel command us to continue, a perpetual memory of that his precious death until his coming again; Hear us, O merciful Father, we beseech thee; and grant that we, receiving these thy creatures of bread and wine, according to thy Son our Saviour Jesus Christ's holy institution, in remembrance of his death and passion, may be partakers of his most blessed body and blood; who, in the same night that he was betrayed, took bread; and when he had given thanks, he brake it, and gave it to his disciples, saying, Take, eat; this is my body which is given for you. Do this in remembrance of me. Likewise after supper he took the cup; and when he had given thanks, he gave it to them, saying, Drink ye all of this; for this is my blood of the New Testament, which is shed for you and for many, for remission of sins: do this as oft as ye shall drink it in remembrance of me.

Then shall the Minister first receive the communion in both kinds himself, and next deliver it to other ministers, if any be there present (that they may help the chief minister), and after to the people in their hands kneeling. And when he delivereth the bread he shall say:

Take and eat this, in remembrance that Christ died for thee, and feed on him in thy heart by faith with thanksgiving.

And the minister that delivereth the cup, shall say:

Drink this in remembrance that Christ's blood was shed for thee, and be thankful.

Then shall the Priest say the Lord's Prayer, the people repeating after him every petition.

After shall be said as followeth:

O Lord and heavenly Father, we thy humble servants entirely desire thy fatherly goodness mercifully to accept this our sacrifice of praise and thanksgiving; most humbly beseeching thee to grant, that by the merits and death of thy Son Jesus Christ, and through faith in his blood, we and all thy whole church may obtain remission of our sins, and all other benefits of his passion. And here we offer and present unto thee, O Lord, ourselves, our souls and bodies, to be a reasonable, holy, and lively sacrifice unto thee; humbly beseeching thee, that all we which be partakers of this holy communion, may be fulfilled with thy grace and heavenly benediction. And although we be unworthy, through our manifold sins to offer unto thee any sacrifice, yet we beseech thee to accept this our bounden duty and service; not weighing our merits, but pardoning our offences, through Jesus Christ our Lord; by whom, and with whom in the unity of the Holy Ghost, all honour and glory be unto thee, O Father Almighty, world without end. Amen.

Or this:

Almighty and everliving God, we most heartily thank thee, for that thou dost vouchsafe to feed us, which have duly received these holy mysteries, with the spiritual food of the most precious body and blood of thy Son our Savior Jesus Christ, and dost assure us thereby of thy favour and goodness towards us, and that we be very members incorporate in thy mystical body, which is the blessed company of all faithful people, and be also heirs through hope of thy

everlasting kingdom, by the merits of the most precious death and passion of thy dear Son: we now most humble beseech thee, O heavenly Father, so to assist us with thy grace, that we may continue in that holy fellowship and do all such good works as thou hast prepared for us to walk in, through Jesus Christ our Lord: to whom, with thee and the Holy Ghost, be all honour and glory, world without end. Amen.

Comment

The Prayer of Consecration of 1552 falls into three parts, even though it was printed as one, long paragraph. The first part is the Declaration and could be said to exhibit in a striking manner the mind of the Protestant Reformers, with its great emphasis upon the unique, sacrificial death of the Lord Jesus Christ. The verb "continue" replaced the "celebrate" of 1549 and "of himself" was added after "oblation" in order to remove any possible ambiguity.

The Petition, from "Hear us..." to "body and blood," is rewritten to remove the *epiclesis* or invocation ("with thy Holy Spirit and Word") and to exclude not only the possibility of understanding the words in terms of transubstantiation but also in terms of the Lutheran doctrine of consubstantiation. Thus the primary change in the Petition from 1549 to 1552 is in terms of prayer being offered for the worshipper rather than a blessing being sought upon the bread.

Finally, the Recital, the consecration proper, is the Gospel record of the Institution by the Lord Jesus Christ, and it is a near perfect blend of the four scriptural accounts (in Matthew, Mark, Luke and 1 Corinthians).

In terms of rubrics there were no instructions given to the Minister in the 1552 Consecration Prayer. The 1549 had three - making the sign of the cross at the *epiclesis* or invocation, taking the bread, and then the cup, into the hands.

Further developments

This 1552 *BCP* became the Prayer Book authorized by Queen Elizabeth I in 1559 for her long reign, after the Roman Rite imposed by Queen Mary had been set aside by the new Settlement of Religion. However, three significant changes were made to the 1552 *BCP* in its becoming the 1559 *BCP*.

First of all, the words of administration of Holy Communion of the 1552 Rite were to be prefixed by those of the 1549 Rite. So communicants heard:

The body of our Lord Jesus Christ which was given for thee, preserve thy body and soul into everlasting life. And take and eat this in remembrance that Christ died for thee, and feed on him in thine heart by faith, with thanksgiving.

The blood of our Lord Jesus Christ which was shed for thee, preserve thy body and soul unto everlasting life. And drink this in remembrance that Christ's blood was shed for thee, and be thankful.

Whatever else this new form of words does it certainly allows for an understanding of the Lord's Supper which makes it more than an exercise in memory!

In the second place, the Black Rubric (quoted above) was dropped. The Church of England - or at least the Queen as its earthly Governor - had no embarrassment or inhibition about kneeling to pray and to receive the sacramental body and blood of Christ at Holy Communion. In fact, this Queen is reported to have said in response to questions about Holy Communion that her own faith could be expressed as:

> His were the words that spake it,
> He took the bread and brake it,
> And what his word doth make it,
> I receive and take it.

"A good start in eucharistic theology," we may want to say!

Thirdly, the famous Ornaments Rubric was introduced at the beginning of Morning Prayer. It was to lead to a variety of interpretations over the next four centuries in the Church of England. The Rubric required that "such Ornaments of the Church, and of the Ministers thereof, at all times of their Ministration, shall be retained, and be in use, as were in this Church of England, by the authority of Parliament, in the Second Year of the Reign of King Edward the Sixth." Was this intended actually to restore eucharistic vestments? Apparently so. The rubrics in the 1549 *BCP* required the Priest to wear "a white, plain Alb" with "a vestment or cope." An assisting deacon was to wear "an alb with tunacle." However, the restoration of vestments was not enforced by Elizabeth or her successors and they were little used in England until the time of the Anglo-Catholic revival in the nineteenth century.

Apart from changes made to the text of the *BCP*, an important development for the actual administration and doctrine of the Holy Communion occurred in the second half of Elizabeth's reign. It was decided (and later enshrined in the Canon Laws of 1603) that if the Minister used all the consecrated bread and wine, then he had actually to repeat the words of Institution of the Prayer of Consecration in connexion with further bread and wine before using it for communion. This means that there was a move from the Calvinist teaching that the words of Institution were said only for the benefit of the receivers; to the Lutheran (and now Anglican) teaching that the words of Institution were both for the elements of bread and wine and the human receivers. The consecration of the elements was clearly now understood to be a necessary part of the eucharistic action, and this was taught by the two apologists for the Church of England, John Jewel and Richard Hooker.

In terms of the understanding of the Presence of Christ in the Sacrament, the clear position was to deny both Roman Catholic transubstantiation and Zwinglian symbolism. But where did the emphasis come between these poles?

In *Article XXVIII* the Church declared:

The Body of Christ is given, taken and eaten, in the Supper, only after an heavenly and spiritual manner. And the mean whereby the Body of Christ is received and eaten in the Supper is Faith.

In his famous *The Laws of Ecclesiastical Polity*, Richard Hooker notes that there are only three expositions of *This is my Body* which deserve serious study.

The first is the Lutheran interpretation:

"This is in itself before participation really and truly the natural substance of My Body by reason of the coexistence which My omnipotent Body hath with the sanctified element of bread."

The second is the Roman Catholic doctrine:

"This is itself and before participation the very true and natural substance of My Body, by force of that Deity which with the Words of Consecration abolisheth the substance of bread and substituteth in the place thereof My Body."

Finally there is the Reformed Catholic or Anglican understanding:

"This hallowed food, through concurrence of divine power, is in verity and truth unto faithful receivers instrumentally a cause of that mystical participation, whereby as I make Myself wholly theirs, so I give them in hand an actual possession of all such saving grace as My sacrificed Body can yield, and as their souls do presently need, this is to them and in them My Body."

This approach was later called Receptionism.

Of the Eucharistic Presence, Hooker wrote:

It is on all sides plainly confessed, *first*, that this sacrament is a true and a real participation of Christ, who thereby imparteth himself, even his whole person as a mystical head, unto every soul that receiveth him; and that every such receiver doth thereby incorporate or unite himself unto Christ as a mystical member of him ... *Secondly*, that to whom the person of Christ is thus communicated, to him he giveth, by the same Sacrament, his Holy Spirit to sanctify them ... *Thirdly*, that what merit, force, and virtue soever there is in his sacrificed body and blood, we freely, fully and wholly have it by this Sacrament. *Fourthly*, that the effect thereof in us, is a real transmutation of our souls and bodies from sin to righteousness ... Christ assisting this heavenly banquet with his personal and true presence, doth, by his own divine power, add to the natural substance thereof supernatural efficacy, which addition to the nature of those consecrated elements, changeth them and maketh them that unto us that which otherwise they could not be; that to us they are thereby made such instruments as mystically yet truly invisibly yet really work our communion or fellowship with the person of Jesus Christ, as well in that he is man as God, our participation also in the fruit, grace, and efficacy of His body and blood, whereupon there seemeth a kind of transubstantiation in us, ... (*Eccesiastical Polity*, Book 5, sec., 67).

As to the eucharistic sacrifice there was virtually nothing said by the Elizabeth divines. They were so intent on not giving any impression of a repetition of the Sacrifice of Calvary that their ears were not open to suggestions that the patristic notion of eucharistic sacrifice did not undermine the unique Sacrifice of Calvary. However, John Jewel, the Apologist, wrote of the Eucharistic Sacrifice in these terms:

The ministration of the Holy Communion is sometimes of the ancient Fathers called an unbloody sacrifice, not in respect of any corporal or fleshly presence, that is imagined to be there without blood-shedding, but for that it representeth and reporteth unto our minds the One and Everlasting Sacrifice that Christ made in His Body upon the Cross ... This remembrance and oblation of praises, and rendering thanks unto God, for our redemption in the blood of Christ, is called of the old Fathers an unbloody Sacrifice and of St. Augustine, the Sacrifice of the new Test. (*Works*, London, 1609, p. 428).

It was left to Anglican writers in the seventeenth century to go in search of and articulate a doctrine of the eucharistic sacrifice as an objective repetition of the memory (*a memorial*) of the Sacrifice of the Cross, a memorial which is offered to God.

When King James I came to the throne, there was no need for a change of religion as there had been in 1559! After listening to Puritan objections to the Elizabethan Prayer Book, he caused minor changes to be made and issued it as revised by his own authority. What James I is best known for, is his agreement with the Puritans that a new translation of the Bible be made. It was! The British call it the Authorized Version of 1611 while Americans usually call it the King James Version.

Facing which way?

Before the Reformation of the sixteenth century the normal English parish church had a square-ended chancel cut off from the nave by a screen. The celebrant, facing East and at the altar which was up to the wall (with his back to the people), was far away from the congregation in the nave. Often they heard little but they did see the elevation of the Host at the consecration.

Cranmer and his fellow reformers sought to remedy this unsatisfactory situation by gaining more involvement of the congregation, whose members were to come up the altar at the offertory to place their gifts in the box or chest and then to remain there in the chancel to receive Communion. This meant that the 1549 *BCP* left the priest celebrating Eastward.

For reformers who were influenced by the Continental Reformation, the minimal revision envisaged by the 1549 Rite was insufficient. So steps were taken to remove altars and replace them with tables and to put the table in that part of the chancel which the congregation could see. Sometimes the long sides of the table faced north and south and sometimes east and west; and the celebrant stood wherever seemed the best place to be seen and heard.

The position was clarified by the 1552 *BCP* with this rubric.

> "The Table having at the Communion time a fair, white linen cloth upon it, shall stand in the body of the church, or in the chancel, where Morning Prayer and Evening Prayer be appointed to be said. And the Priest standing at the north side of the Table, shall say..."

This arrangement was confirmed and endorsed by the Prayer Book and Royal Injunctions of 1559; and thus, became the general practice in England in the reigns of Elizabeth I and James I. There were problems with this arrangement. One obvious one was that, since the naves of churches were used for all kinds of meetings in the days before church halls, the "holy" Table was used for "unholy" purposes - to the horror of sensitive souls. Therefore, when William Laud became Archbishop of Canterbury he caused churches to place the Table by the East wall in the chancel, to erect rails around it, and to direct that Communion be served as people knelt at the rails. However, the Northward celebration continued until the disruption of the Church of England during the Commonwealth and Protectorate, and then it continued after the Restoration of the Monarchy in 1662.

CHAPTER FIVE

A New Uniformity: the 1662 BCP

Much happened within and to English religion in the seventeenth century. The religious and moral power of Puritanism, which was partially suppressed by Elizabeth I and James I, exerted itself with great success in the latter part of the reign of Charles I. So much so that Charles I was executed and the Established Church of England took on a very different form during the 1640s and 1650s. The *Book of Common Prayer* was prohibited and the Bishops had no official position in the period when England had no resident king (1649-1660). In fact, Cromwell set up a new National Church in the 1650s in place of the old Episcopal administration (see Peter Toon, "The Cromwellian National Church," in *Puritans and Calvinism*, 1972).

A Puritan was essentially someone (minister or layman) who wished to purify the National Church more fully and particularly according to Reformed (= Calvinist or Presbyterian) principles. Theologically, the great doctrinal and liturgical monuments of English Puritanism are the Confession of Faith, the Catechisms and the Directory for Public Worship, which were produced in the Jerusalem Chamber of Westminster Abbey in the mid-1640s. These documents went north and were adopted by the National (Presbyterian) Church of Scotland, but they were soon forgotten in England as Puritanism, as a political force, disintegrated, and Charles II returned to the throne in 1660.

One (but by no means the only) reason why the Puritans were opposed to the Royalist Church of England was because they believed that in the 1630s the Archbishop of Canterbury, William Laud, had deliberately taken actions to push the Church of England closer to Roman Catholic practice and ceremonial.

> It was a commonplace of Puritan polemic that Laud had tampered with the text of the Prayer Book, but only two instances were produced: that he had changed the opening of the Prayer for the Royal Family, and that he had substituted "*at* the name of Jesus" for "in." As archbishop he concentrated his attention, liturgically speaking, on placing the altar [table] against the east wall of the chancel, fencing it with rails, making the communicants come to the altar to receive, and reading the Ante-Communion [the service up to the Exhortations] at the altar, not in the reading-pew. These directions combined with the Canons to produce the typical Laudian sanctuary, the altar with a silk or velvet carpet falling loose at the corners, richly carved altar-rails, and the floor paved with marble in black and white squares (G. J.Cuming, *A History of Anglican Liturgy*, 1982, p.107).

Laud was also associated with the attempt to force upon Scotland a more "catholic" Prayer Book than the English *BCP* in 1637. The introduction of the Book led to rioting, and it was withdrawn.

During the ascendancy of the Puritans, many English Christians used the *Book of Common Prayer* in their homes and for private devotions. In the parish churches, some clergy used it for public worship in the sense that, knowing its content off by heart, they spoke it as if it were their own free prayer. Other clergy, who had specific interests in liturgy, made use of their enforced leisure to work on suggestions for the perfection of the Cranmerian *Book of Common Prayer*. Some of these went into the English 1662 and the Scottish 1764 Books.

The Restoration

After the Civil War and the Commonwealth and Protectorate, England witnessed the restoration of the monarchy
and of the episcopate as well as worship ordered by the
Book of Common Prayer. This 1662 Book is essentially that
of 1604 (and thus also of 1559).

At the Savoy Conference in July 1661, the Presbyterian
Puritans on the one side pressed for a more "Protestant"
Book (in terms of both content and rubrics) while the
Laudians on the other side hoped for a more "Catholic" Book.
What the Laudians wanted in the Service of Holy Commun-
ion were the following changes or additions:

1. To substitute "Catholic Church" for "Church Militant here
    in earth" in the introduction to the Prayer for the Church
    in order to allow for prayer for the dead to be included.

2. To enlarge the Eucharistic Prayer by (a) including an In-
    vocation of the Holy Spirit and Word upon the Bread and
    Wine; (b) placing a "Memorial or Prayer of Oblation" im-
    mediately after the Prayer of Consecration - "We thy
    humble servants do celebrate and make here before thy
    Divine Majesty, with these thy holy gifts, the Memorial
    which thy Son hath willed and commanded us to
    make...death of thy Son, Jesus Christ, now represented
    unto Thee;" (c) adding "that whosoever shall be partakers
    of this Holy Communion may worthily receive the most
    precious body and blood of thy Son, Jesus Christ."

3. To sing the *Agnus Dei* during the Administration.

4. The Table always to stand in the East.

5. The Priest "to offer up and place" the Bread and Wine on
    the Table.

6. Wafer bread to be allowed.

These desired changes or additions, are generally in line
with the contents of the 1549 *BCP* and the 1637 Scottish
BCP.

The motivation for these proposals, and the reason why their proposers and supporters felt so strongly about them, was that they were seen to be an essential part of the liturgies from the Early Church. These liturgies had been carefully studied in the seventeenth century by both English and Scottish "Laudians," and they had come to the conclusion that the Offering, Oblation, and Invocation were necessary for a genuine or true Eucharistic Prayer in the one, holy, catholic Church. Their convictions were to be expressed and find a permanent home in the later Scottish and American *Books of Common Prayer.* It would be wrong, however, to think that they did not believe that the Consecration Prayer in the 1604 and 1662 Books was valid. They certainly saw it as valid but lacking wholeness. It was true but not the whole truth; it was satisfactory but not excellent. They judged the 1604 Book by patristic norms. Those who defended the 1604 (thus 1552 and 1559) argued for simplicity, for carefully following the biblical accounts of the Lord's Supper in the Gospels and I Corinthians, and for general not specific guidance from the early centuries.

The mood in Convocation in 1661 was to keep the Church of England a reformed Catholic Church and truly the Church of the whole nation. Thus, there were many minor, cosmetic changes (e.g., "the creed sung or said" instead of merely "said," and "The Lord's Table" for "God's board").

As a concession to the more Protestant Churchmen, the Black Rubric (with a few verbal changes) concerning kneeling was restored from the 1552 Book. As concessions to the Laudians were the addition of remembrance of the faithful dead in the Prayer for the Church, the words "pronounce this absolution" for "say this" after the confession of sins, the use of the words "Paten" and "Chalice", the expression "The Prayer of Consecration," a rubric before this Prayer directing the ordering of Bread and Wine, and the "Amen" at the end of the Prayer of Consecration.

The contents of the 1662 Order for Holy Communion are as follows:

The Lord's Prayer
The Collect for Purity
The Ten Commandments
The Collects for the King
The Collect of the Day
The Epistle
The Gospel
The Creed
The Notices
The Sermon
The Offertory Sentences
The Placing of the Bread and Wine
The Prayer for the Church
The Exhortations
The Invitation
The Confession
The Absolution
The Comfortable Words
The *Sursum Corda*
Prefaces
The *Sanctus*
The Prayer of Humble Access
The Prayer of Consecration
The Words of Administration
The Lord's Prayer
The Thanksgiving (Choice from Two)
The *Gloria in Excelsis*
The Blessing

The rubrics assume that the Minister of the Sacrament shall celebrate from the North side (the left side from the perspective of the congregation) at the holy Table which is up against the East wall and that the communicants will come forward from the nave into the chancel to receive, kneeling at the rails.

The Prayer of Consecration and its Context

After which the Priest shall proceed, saying:

           Lift up your hearts.
Answer: **We lift them up unto the Lord.**

Priest: **Let us give thanks unto our Lord God.**
Answer: **It is meet and right so to do.**

Then shall the Priest turn to the Lord's Table, and say:

It is very meet, right, and our bounden duty, that we should at all times and in all places, give thanks unto thee, O Lord, Holy Father, Almighty, Everlasting God.

Here shall follow, the proper Preface, according to the time, if there be any specially appointed: or else immediately shall follow:

Therefore with Angels and Archangels, and with all the company of heaven, we laud and magnify thy glorious Name, evermore praising thee, and saying, Holy, holy, holy, Lord God of Hosts, heaven and earth are full of thy Glory: Glory be to thee, O Lord most High.   Amen.

Then shall the Priest kneeling down at the Lord's Table, say in the name of all them that shall receive the Communion, this Prayer following.

We do not presume to come to this thy Table, O merciful Lord, trusting in our own righteousness, but in thy manifold and great mercies.   We are not worthy so much as to gather up the crumbs under thy Table.   But thou art the same Lord, whose property is always to have mercy: grant us therefore, gracious Lord, so to eat the flesh of thy dear Son Jesus Christ, and to drink his blood, that our sinful bodies may be made clean by his body, and our souls washed through his most precious blood, and that we may evermore dwell in him, and he in us. Amen.

When the Priest, standing before the Table, hath so ordered the Bread and Wine, that he may with the more readiness and decency break the Bread before the people, and take the Cup into his hands, he shall say the Prayer of Consecration, as followeth.

Almighty God, our heavenly Father, who of thy tender mercy didst give thine only Son Jesus Christ to suffer death upon the Cross for our redemption; who made there (by his one oblation of himself once offered) a full, perfect, and sufficient sacrifice, oblation, and satisfaction, for the sins of the whole world; and did institute, and in his holy Gospel command us to continue, a perpetual memory of that his precious death, until his coming again; Hear us, 0 merciful Father, we most humbly beseech thee; and grant that we receiving these thy creatures of bread and wine, according to thy Son our Saviour Jesus Christ's holy institution, in remembrance of his death and passion, may be partakers of his most blessed Body and Blood: who in the same night that he was betrayed, *(a)* took Bread; and, when he had given thanks, *(b)* he brake it, and gave it to his disciples, saying, Take, eat; *(c)* this is my Body which is given for you: Do this in remembrance of me. Likewise after supper *(d)* he took the Cup; and, when he had given thanks, he gave it to them, saying, Drink ye all of this; for *(e)* this is my Blood of the New Testament, which is shed for you and for many for the remission of sins: Do this, as oft as ye shall drink it, in remembrance of me. *Amen.*

[Manual acts are required at a,b,c,d & e.]

Then shall the Minister first receive the Communion in both kinds himself, and then proceed to deliver the same to the Bishops, Priests, and Deacons, in like manner (if any be present), and after that to the people also in order, into their hands, all meekly kneeling. And, when he delivereth the Bread to any One, he shall say,

The Body of our Lord Jesus Christ, which was given for thee, preserve thy body and soul unto everlasting life: Take and eat this in remembrance that Christ died for thee, and feed on him in thy heart by faith with thanksgiving.

And the Minister that delivereth the Cup to any one shall say,

The Blood of our Lord Jesus Christ, which was shed for thee, preserve thy body and soul unto everlasting life: Drink this in remembrance that Christ's blood was shed for thee, and be thankful.

If the consecrated Bread or Wine be all spent before all have communicated, the Priest is to consecrate more, according to the Form before prescribed: Beginning at [Our Saviour Christ in the same night, etc.] *for the blessing of the Bread; and at [Likewise after Supper, etc.] for the blessing of the Cup.*

When all have communicated, the Minister shall return to the Lord's Table, and reverently place upon it what remaineth of the consecrated Elements, covering the same with a fair linen cloth. Then shall the Priest say the Lord's Prayer, the people repeating after him every Petition.

Comment

The publication of the 1662 *BCP* represents the climax of a development which began in 1549. Cranmer's English Rite was "protestantized" by Edward VI, proscribed by Queen Mary, prescribed in modified form by Elizabeth, James I and Charles I and then reissued by Charles II. Since 1662 it has been used in many countries and translated into many languages. It is one of the treasures of the English language and represents one of the great liturgical and devotional books of the Christian Church.

The well-known liturgical expert, E. C. Ratcliff wrote of the Archbishop:

Cranmer was the master, or rather the creator, of English liturgical style, because he had apprehended the nature of worship. To serve the purposes of worship he brought the resources of the scholar: appreciation of the fine compositions of liturgical Latin; knowledge of the rules of rhythm and clausula; facility and felicity in transition; a feeling for the meanings of words. With such resources, and moved by a profound religious sincerity, Cranmer made of English a liturgical language comparable with Latin at its best.

'The ink of the scholar', so runs an Arabic proverb, 'is of more worth than the blood of the martyr.' The proverb is true of Cranmer. In his liturgy he bequeathed to the newly reformed English Church an instrument of worship which was to ensure to it a principle of life, and which also, in its remarkable combination of the traditional with the contemporary, of the old with the new, was to be not the least important factor in imparting to Anglican Christianity its distinctive stamp. (*Liturgical Studies*, 1976, p. 199.)

For those who wish to be Reformed Catholics, rather than Protestants or Roman Catholics, its use still provides the very best way of fulfilling that desire. With the actual *BCP* is bound the *Ordinal* (the ordination services) and this book of services makes clear that there is no parity of Ministers (as the Puritans argued). Rather there are truly three distinct orders, those of bishop, priest and deacon. In fact, to understand the office and function of ministers within the *BCP* it is necessary to read and follow the content of the *Ordinal*.

In America, where so many congregations, families, and individual persons are on "the liturgical trail" out of a narrow Protestantism in search of "the early Church" and "the best of the Reformation," the 1662 *BCP* with the *Ordinal* and with the *Thirty-Nine Articles of Religion* (all bound together in one compact book) represents an excellent end to their pilgrimage and search (if they also find a godly Bishop!). If they use the 1662 Book as printed they will need of course to change the prayers and ask God for blessing upon America rather than England!

The Canadian 1959 Book

As an alternative to the English *Book of Common Prayer* of 1662, there stands the Canadian *Book of Common Prayer* (1959/1962). The Order of the Service up to the *Sursum Corda* is that of 1662. From there it is as follows:

The *Sursum Corda*
The Proper Preface
The *Sanctus*
The Prayer of Consecration (longer than 1662)
The Peace (said as the congregation kneels)
"We do not presume..."
The Communion (singing of the *Agnus Dei* optional)
The Lord's Prayer
The Thanksgiving
The *Gloria in Excelsis*
The Blessing

The "Blessed is he that cometh in the Name of the Lord: Hosanna in the highest" is optional and may be used either before the Prayer of Consecration or before the Communion. The "Peace" is the ancient form - "The Peace of the Lord be always with you: (*people*) and with thy spirit."

In the Canadian Book can be seen some of the fruit of the early Anglican (in contrast to the later, post-Vatican II) liturgical movement. This movement had been frustrated in not being able to see within the Church of England the revision of the 1662 Book known as the 1928 Book - a revision which was accepted by the Convocation of the Church of England but rejected by its ancient House of Laity, the House of Commons. In the revision of the Canadian 1962 Book, some of the aims of this early, conservative movement are seen. At the offertory, the Priest is directed to present [to the Lord] and place on the Table the bread and wine. The "Blessed is he that cometh..." and "the Peace" and the "O Lamb of God..." are introduced and the Prayer of Consecration is extended to include a Memorial, Invocation and Oblation. However, the Black Rubric is retained.

The extended Prayer of Consecration is as follows:

Blessing and glory and thanksgiving be unto thee Almighty God, our heavenly Father, who of thy tender mercy didst give thine only Son Jesus Christ to take our nature upon him, and to suffer death upon the Cross for our redemption; who made there, by his one oblation of himself once offered, a full, perfect, and sufficient sacrifice, oblation and satisfaction, for the sins of the whole world; and did insti-

tute, and in his holy Gospel command us to continue, a perpetual memorial of that his precious death, until his coming again.

Hear us, O merciful Father, we most humbly beseech thee; and grant that we receiving these thy creatures of bread and wine, according to thy Son our Saviour Jesus Christ's holy institution, in remembrance of his death and passion, may be partakers of his most blessed Body and Blood; who, in the same night that he was betrayed *(a)* took Bread; and, when he had given thanks, *(b)* he brake it; and gave it to his disciples, saying, Take eat; *(c)* this is my Body which is given for you: Do this in remembrance of me. Likewise after supper *(d)* he took the Cup; and, when he had given thanks, he gave it to them, saying, Drink ye all of this; for *(e)* this is my Blood of the new Covenant, which is shed for you and for many for the remission of sins: Do this, as oft as ye shall drink it, in remembrance of me.

Wherefore, O Father, Lord of heaven and earth, we thy humble servants, with all thy holy Church, remembering the precious death of thy beloved Son, his mighty resurrection, and glorious ascension, and looking for his coming again in glory, do make before thee, in this sacrament of the holy Bread of eternal life and the Cup of everlasting salvation, the memorial which he hath commanded; And we entirely desire thy fatherly goodness mercifully to accept this our sacrifice of praise and thanksgiving, most humbly beseeching thee to grant, that by the merits and death of thy Son Jesus Christ, and through faith in his blood, we and all thy whole Church may obtain remission of our sins, and all other benefits of his passion; and we pray that by the power of the Holy Spirit, all we who are partakers of this holy Communion may be fulfilled with thy grace and heavenly benediction; through Jesus Christ our Lord, by whom and with whom, in the unity of the Holy Spirit, all honour and glory be unto thee, O Father Almighty, world without end. *Amen.*

[Manual acts are required at a,b,c,d, & e.]

CHAPTER SIX

A Scottish Innovation: the 1764 Communion Office

American Episcopalians (Anglicans) have special ties to Scotland and to the small Episcopal Church there. In Scotland, the National Church is, of course, not Anglican but Presbyterian. From the Scottish Episcopal Church, the Episcopal Church of the USA derived both part of her Episcopate and the more essential features of her Eucharistic Prayer.

In his outstanding book on the Scottish Rite of 1764, John Dowden, once Bishop of Edinburgh, wrote this:

> The *Scottish Communion Office*, as the Eucharistic Service-book peculiar to the Scottish Church is designated, was not the work of one man or of one age. It was not produced hastily, but by a gradual development attained its present form. It is ultimately traceable to perhaps a greater variety of sources than any known liturgy. The Churches of Eastern and Western Christendom, early, medieval, and modern times have all contributed towards determining its structure or supplying its content. Yet it is not disfigured by the signs of patchwork, but possesses the unity and beauty of a living thing. It is an outcome of the patient and reverent study of Christian antiquity; but it is conceived in no mere antiquarian spirit, and is no product of a dilettante affectation of the antique. Like everything that lives, it came into being from a living impulse; but also, like everything that lives, it was sensitive

to its actual environment and exhibited the living power of adapting itself to that environment without permanent detriment to its life. It is framed upon primitive models, and breathes the spirit of primitive devotion, while experience continually demonstrates its suitability to the needs of the living Church (*The Scottish Communion Office 1764*, 1888 [new ed.,1922], p.1).

This is praise indeed from one who not only had studied its history but had also absorbed its spirituality.

For those who think that Cranmer was on the right lines with his 1549 *Book of Common Prayer* and that the 1552 was a move away from primitive, patristic models towards too much of an accommodation with the theology of Continental Protestantism, the Scottish Rite is obviously very attractive. In fact, the main sources from which the *Communion Office* was constructed are: (1) certain Greek Liturgies and liturgical writings; (2) The 1549 and 1662 English *Books of Common Prayer*; (3) The Scottish *Book of Common Prayer*, 1637; and (4) The Communion Offices of the Nonjurors, particularly that one entitled, *A Communion Office taken partly from the Primitive Liturgies and partly from the first English Reformed Prayer Book* (1718).

The 1637 Book of Common Prayer

The Scottish Book of 1637, commonly but mistakenly known as "Laud's Prayer Book," was read for the first time in St Giles's Cathedral, Edinburgh on July 23, 1637. Rioting broke out against both the King and the Church: the Book was withdrawn. The text of the service up to the offertory is much the same as that of 1559/1604, except that (for Scottish ears) the priest is called the presbyter.

After the printing of the offertory sentences there is the following rubric:

While the Presbyter distinctly pronounceth some or all of these sentences for the offertory, the Deacon...shall receive the devotions of the people there present in a bason for that purpose. And when all have offered, he shall reverently bring the said bason with the oblations therein, and deliver it to the Presbyter, who shall humbly present it before the Lord, and set it upon the holy Table. And the Presbyter shall then offer up and place the bread and wine prepared for the Sacrament upon the Lord's Table, that it may be ready for that service...

The offering up of the gifts of bread and wine is not found in the 1549 *BCP*; rather, it is found in the ancient Greek liturgies. Also, the rubric restores to the Deacon one of his ancient duties.

Following the offertory there is the Prayer for the whole state of Christ's Church militant here in earth. Its content is less than that of 1549 but more than that of 1552: that is, it seeks to commemorate the dead in Christ without appearing to pray for the dead, or ask for the intercession of the saints. After this Prayer comes the Exhortation, followed by, "You that do truly and earnestly...," the Confession of Sins, the Absolution and the Comfortable Words.

The Eucharistic Prayer proceeds with the *Sursum Corda*, the Proper Preface, the *Sanctus*, the 1604 Prayer of Consecration (with the manual acts) into which is inserted the *epiclesis* or invocation in these words: "...and of thy almighty goodness vouchsafe so to bless and sanctify with thy word and holy Spirit these thy gifts and creatures of bread and wine, that they may be unto us the body and blood of thy most dearly beloved Son." This is followed immediately by the Prayer of Oblation:

Wherefore O Lord and heavenly Father, according to the institution of thy dearly beloved Son our Saviour Jesus Christ, we thy humble servants do celebrate and make here before thy divine Majesty, with these thy holy gifts, the memorial which thy Son hath commanded us to make, having in remembrance his blessed passion, mighty resurrection, and glorious ascension, rendering unto thee most hearty thanks for the innumerable benefits procured unto us by the same. And we entirely...

Then came the Lord's Prayer, the "We do not presume...," followed by the Communion. The words of 1549 not 1552 were used at the Administration. After Communion the second Prayer of Thanksgiving from 1604 was offered, followed by the *Gloria in Excelsis* and the Blessing.

In summary, it may be said that the major differences between the traditional English Rite (1552, 1559, 1604) and the Scottish Rite of 1637 are these: (1) The benediction of the gifts of bread and wine by the invocation of the Holy Spirit (in the Scottish but not in the English Book); (2) The prayer of Oblation (as part of the Eucharistic Prayer in the Scottish but after Communion in a briefer form in the English Book); (3) The specific commemoration of the faithful departed in the Scottish Prayer for the Church, but not found in the English Prayer; (4) The removal of the second clause of the 1662 Book in the words of Administration of the Communion in the Scottish Book; and (5) the use of the King James Version of the Bible (1611) in the Scottish Book.

The contents of the *1764 Scottish Communion Office* are as follows:

The Lord's Prayer
The Collect for Purity
The Ten Commandments or the Summary of the Law
Prayer for grace to keep the Commandments
Prayer for the King
The Collect of the Day
The Epistle
The Gospel
The Creed
A Sermon
The Exhortation
Presentation of offerings with Scripture sentences
(the rubric in 1764 here is that of 1637, quoted above)
The *Sursum Corda*
The Proper Preface
The *Sanctus*
The Canon in Three Parts
The Consecration
The Oblation
The Invocation

The Prayer for the whole state of Christ's Church
The Lord's Prayer
"Ye that do truly and earnestly..."
The General Confession
The Absolution
The Comfortable Words
"We do not presume..."
The Communion (with the 1549 words of Administration)
The Prayer of Thanksgiving
The *Gloria in Excelsis*
The Blessing

Having seen the general layout it is now appropriate to look at the actual words of the Rite from the offertory onwards:

While the Presbyter distinctly pronounceth some or all of these sentences for the offertory, the Deacon, or (if no such be Present) some other fit person, shall receive the devotions of the people there present, in a bason provided for that purpose. And when all have offered, he shall reverently bring the said bason, with the oblations therein, and deliver it to the Presbyter; who shall humbly present it before the Lord, and set it upon the holy table, saying,

BLESSED be thou, O Lord God, for ever and ever. Thine, O Lord, is the greatness, and the glory, and the victory, and the majesty: for all that is in the heaven and in the earth is thine : thine is the kingdom, O Lord, and thou art exalted as head above all : both riches and honour come of thee, and of thine own do we give unto thee. *Amen.*

And the Presbyter shall then offer up, and place the bread and wine prepared for the sacrament upon the Lord's table; and shall say,

	The Lord be with you.
Answer.	**And with thy spirit.**
Presbyter.	**Lift up your hearts.**
Answer.	**We lift them up unto the Lord.**
Presbyter.	**Let us give thanks unto our Lord God.**
Answer.	**It is meet and right so to do.**

Presbyter. **It is very meet, right, and our bounden duty, that we should at all times, and in all places, give thanks unto thee, O Lord, Almighty, everlasting God.**

Here shall follow the Proper preface, according to the time, if there be any especially appointed ; or else immediately shall follow,

Therefore with angels and archangels, and with all the company of heaven, we laud and magnify thy glorious name, evermore praising thee, and saying, Holy, holy, holy Lord God of hosts, heaven and earth are full of thy glory, Glory be to thee, O Lord most high. Amen.

Then the Presbyter standing at such a part of the holy table as he may with most ease and decency use both his hands, shall say the prayer of consecration, as followeth.

All glory be to thee, Almighty God, our heavenly Father, for that thou of thy tender mercy didst give thy only Son Jesus Christ to suffer death upon the cross for our redemption; who (by his own oblation of himself once offered) made a full, perfect and sufficient sacrifice, oblation and satisfaction, for the sins of the whole world, and did institute, and in his holy gospel command us to continue a perpetual memorial of that his precious death and sacrifice until his coming again. For in the night that he was betrayed (a) he took bread; and when he had given thanks, (b) he brake it, and gave it to his disciples, saying, Take, eat, (c) THIS IS MY BODY, which is given for you: DO this in remembrance of me. Likewise after supper (d) he took the cup; and when he had given thanks, he gave it to them, saying, Drink ye all of this, for (e) THIS IS MY BLOOD, of the new testament, which is shed for you and for many, for the remission of sins : DO this as oft as ye shall drink it in remembrance of me.

[There are manual acts at a,b,c,d, & e.]

The Oblation

WHEREFORE, O Lord, and heavenly Father, according to the institution of thy dearly beloved Son our Saviour Jesus Christ, we thy humble servants do celebrate and make here before thy divine majesty, with these thy holy gifts, WHICH WE NOW OFFER UNTO THEE, the memorial thy Son hath Commanded us to make ; having in remembrance his blessed passion, and precious death, his mighty resurrection, and glorious ascension ; rendering unto thee most hearty thanks for the innumerable benefits procured unto us by the same.

The Invocation

And we most humbly beseech thee, O merciful Father, to hear us, and of thy almighty goodness vouchsafe to bless and sanctify, with thy word and Holy Spirit, these thy gifts and creatures of bread and wine, that they may become the body and blood of thy most dearly beloved Son. And we earnestly desire thy fatherly goodness, mercifully to accept this our sacrifice of praise and thanksgiving, most humbly beseeching thee to grant, that by the merits and death of thy Son Jesus Christ, and through faith in his blood, we (and all thy whole church) may obtain remission of our sins, and all other benefits of his passion. And here we humbly offer and present unto thee, O Lord, ourselves, our souls and bodies, to be a reasonable, holy and lively sacrifice unto thee, beseeching thee, that whosoever shall be partakers of this holy Communion, may worthily receive the most precious body and blood of thy Son Jesus Christ, and be filled with thy grace and heavenly benediction, and made one body with him, that he may dwell in them, and they in him. And although we are unworthy, through our manifold sins, to offer unto thee any sacrifice; yet we beseech thee to accept this our bounden duty and service, not weighing our merits, but pardoning our offences, through Jesus our Lord: by whom, and with whom, in the unity of the Holy Ghost, all honour and glory be unto thee, O Father Almighty, world without end. *Amen.*

Let us pray for the whole state of Christ's church.

ALMIGHTY and everliving God, who by thy holy Apostle hast taught us to make prayers and supplications, and to give thanks for all men; We humbly beseech thee most mercifully to accept our alms and oblations, and to receive these our prayers, which we offer unto thy divine Majesty; beseeching thee to inspire continually the universal church with the spirit of truth, unity, and concord: and grant that all they that do confess thy holy name, may agree in the truth of thy holy word, and live in unity and godly love. We beseech thee also to save and defend all Christian Kings, Princes, and Governors, and especially thy servant our King, that under him we may be godly and quietly governed: and grant unto his whole council and to all who are put in authority under him, that they may truly and indifferently minister justice, to the punishment of wickedness and vice, and to the maintenance of thy true religion and virtue. Give grace, O heavenly Father, to all Bishops, Priests, and Deacons, that they may both by their life and doctrine set forth thy true and lively word, and rightly and duly administer thy holy sacraments: and to all thy people give thy heavenly grace, that with meek heart, and due reverence, they may hear and receive thy holy word, truly serving thee in holiness and righteousness all the days of their life. And we commend especially to thy merciful goodness the congregation which is here assembled in thy name, to celebrate the commemoration of the most precious death and sacrifice of thy Son and our Saviour Jesus Christ. And we most humbly beseech thee of thy goodness, O Lord, to comfort and succour all those who in this transitory life are in trouble, sorrow, need, sickness, or any other adversity. And we also bless thy holy name for all thy servants, who, having finished their course in faith, do now rest from their labours. And we yield unto thee most high praise and hearty thanks, for the wonderful grace and virtue declared in all thy saints, who have been the choice vessels of thy grace, and the lights of the world in their several generations : most humbly beseeching thee to give us grace to follow the example of their stedfastness in thy faith, and obedience to thy holy commandments, that at the day of the general resurrection, we, and all they who are of the mystical body of thy Son, may be set on his right hand, and hear that his most joyful voice, Come, ye blessed of my Father, inherit the kingdom prepared for you from the foundation of the world. Grant this, O Father, for Jesus Christ's sake, our only Mediator and Advocate. Amen.

Then shall the Presbyter say,

As our Saviour Christ hath commanded and taught us, we are bold to say, Our Father...

Then the Presbyter shall say to them that come to receive the holy communion, this invitation.

Ye that do truly and earnestly repent you of your sins, and are in love and charity with your neighbours, and intend to lead a new life, following the commandments of God, and walking from henceforth in his holy ways; Draw near, and take this holy sacrament to your comfort; and make your humble confession to Almighty God.

Then shall this general confession be made, by the people, along with the Presbyter; he first kneeling down.

Almighty God, Father of our Lord Jesus Christ, maker of all things, judge of all men; We acknowledge and bewail our manifold sins and wickedness, which we from time to time most grievously have committed, by thought, word, and deed, against thy divine Majesty; provoking most justly thy wrath and indignation against us. We do earnestly repent, and are heartily sorry for these our misdoings; the remembrance of them is grievous unto us; the burden of them is intolerable. Have mercy upon us, have mercy upon us, most merciful Father; for thy Son our Lord Jesus Christ's sake, forgive us all that is past; and grant that we may ever hereafter serve and please thee, in newness of life, to the honour and glory of thy name, through Jesus Christ our Lord. Amen.

Then shall the Presbyter, or the Bishop (being present), stand up, and, turning himself to the people, pronounce the absolution, as followeth.

Almighty God, our heavenly Father, who, of his great mercy, hath promised forgiveness of sins to all them who with hearty repentance and true faith turn unto him; Have mercy upon you; pardon and deliver you from all your sins; confirm and strengthen you in all goodness ; and bring you to everlasting life, through Jesus Christ our Lord. *Amen.*

Then shall the Presbyter also say,

Hear what comfortable words our Saviour Christ saith unto all that truly turn to him.

Come unto me, all ye that labour, and are heavy laden, and I will give you rest. Matt. xi. 28.

God so loved the world, that he gave his only begotten Son, that whosoever believeth in him, should not perish, but have everlasting life. John iii. 16.

Hear also what St. Paul saith.

This is a faithful saying, and worthy of all acceptation, that Christ Jesus came into the world to save sinners. I Tim. i. 15.

Hear also what St. John saith.

If any man sin, we have an advocate with the Father, Jesus Christ the righteous : and he is the propitiation for our sins. *I John* ii. 1-2.

Then shall the Presbyter, turning him to the altar, kneel down, and say, in the name of all them that shall communicate, this collect of humble access to the holy communion, as followeth.

We do not presume to come to this thy holy table, O merciful Lord, trusting in our own righteousness, but in thy manifold and great mercies. We are not worthy so much as to gather up the crumbs under thy table: But thou art the same Lord, whose property is always to have mercy. Grant us therefore, gracious Lord, so to eat the flesh of thy clear Son Jesus Christ, and to drink his blood, that our sinful bodies may be made clean by his most sacred body, and our souls washed through his most precious blood, and that we may evermore dwell in him, and he in us. *Amen.*

Then shall the Bishop, if he be present, or else the Presbyter that celebrateth, first receive the communion in both kinds himself, and next deliver it to other Bishops, Presbyters, and Deacons, (if there be any present), and after to the People, in due order, all humbly kneeling. And when he receiveth himself, or delivereth the sacrament of the body of Christ to others, he shall say,

The body of our Lord Jesus Christ, which was given for thee, preserve thy soul and body unto everlasting life.

Here the person receiving shall say, **Amen.**

And the Presbyter or Minister that receiveth the cup himself, or delivereth it to others, shall say this benediction.

The blood of our Lord Jesus Christ, which was shed for thee, preserve thy soul and body unto everlasting life.

Here the person receiving shall say, **Amen.**

If the consecrated bread or wine be all spent before all have communicated, the Presbyter is to consecrate more, according to the form before prescribed, beginning at the words, **All glory be to thee, &c.** *and ending with the words,* **that they may become the body and blood of thy most dearly beloved Son.**

When all have communicated, he that celebrates shall go to the Lord's table, and cover with a fair linen cloth that which remaineth of the consecrated elements, and then say,

Having now received the precious body, and blood of Christ, let us give thanks to our Lord God, who hath graciously vouchsafed to admit us to the participation of his holy mysteries; and let us beg of him grace to perform our vows, and to persevere in our good resolutions; And that being made holy, we may obtain everlasting life, through the merits of the all-sufficient sacrifice of our Lord and Saviour Jesus Christ.

Then the Presbyter shall say this collect of thanksgiving as followeth.

ALMIGHTY and everliving God, we most heartily thank thee, for that thou dost vouchsafe to feed us, who have duly received these holy mysteries, with the spiritual food of the most precious body and blood of thy Son our Saviour Jesus Christ; and dost assure us thereby of thy favour and goodness towards us, and that we are very members incorporate in the mystical body of thy Son, which is the blessed company of all faithful people, and are also heirs through hope of thy everlasting kingdom, by the merits of his most precious death and passion. We now humbly beseech thee, O heavenly Father, so to assist us with thy grace and Holy Spirit, that we may continue in that holy communion and fellowship, and do all such good works as thou hast commanded for us to walk in, through Jesus Christ our Lord; to whom, with the Father and the Holy Ghost, be all honour and glory, world without end. *Amen.*

Comment

There is obviously no rubric requiring the Mixed Chalice as in the 1549 Rite. However, it would appear that such was the custom in Scotland from the seventeenth century.

Bishop Dowden had these comments on the Eucharistic Sacrifice:

The Scottish Office unquestionably brings out into clearer view than the English [1662] that aspect of the Eucharistic celebration in which it is presented as the Church's perpetual memorial of the great Sacrifice of the Cross. As to the nature of the Presence it is as silent as the English. Its language is large and comprehensive. There is no doctrinal belief compatible with the doctrine of the Church of England which is not consonant with the teaching of the Scottish Communion Office. It would be an evil day should any Church of the Anglican Communion adopt a formula of devotion, the language of which was in any sense exclusive of the doctrinal teaching which has the substantial *consensus* of her greatest doctors. It is certainly not so with the Scottish Church. Take, for instance, the classic sentence of [Richard] Hooker [in his *Ecclesiastical Polity*] - "The real presence of Christ's most blessed body and blood is not to be sought for in the sacrament, but in the worthy receiver of the sacrament"; the belief here expressed is in the fullest sense compatible with the Scottish Communion Office. (*The Scottish Communion Office 1764*, p. 7.)

Dowden also believed that by consecration the bread and wine could be said "to be" or "to have been made" or "to have become" the Body of Blood of Christ, in the sense that Jesus Christ intended when he said his words of institution. This is a *realist* understanding of the Presence.

Earlier Archbishop Laud had written these lines on the Eucharistic Sacrifice:

As Christ offered himself once for all, a full and all-sufficient sacrifice for the sin of the whole world, so did he institute and command a memory of this sacrifice in a sacrament, even till his coming again. For, at and in the Eucharist, we offer up to God three sacrifices. One by the priest only; that is the commemorative sacrifice of Christ's death, represented in bread broken and wine poured out. Another by the priest and people jointly; and that is, the sacrifice of praise and thanksgiving for all the benefits and graces we receive by the precious death of Christ. The third, by every particular man for himself only; and that is, the sacrifice of every man's body and soul, to serve him in both all the rest of his life, for this blessing thus bestowed on him. (*Works*, 1847, Vol. 2, p 339.)

The Scottish attitude towards the English 1662 Rite for Holy Communion was much like that of the Nonjurors. It was not so much wrong as deficient. It needed to be supplemented by material based on the ancient Greek Liturgies. Looking back, we may say that the 1764 Rite, as that of 1549, bear eloquent testimony to the desire of the Anglican mind to be faithful to Scripture, but to be so with the guidance and in the spirit of the early Fathers. However, there is not much likelihood of any American Anglican Church wanting to revive the 1764 Rite, primarily because its essential principles have passed into the American 1928 Rite.

CHAPTER SEVEN

The American Rite: the 1928 BCP

We trace the 1928 *BCP* back via the American 1892 *BCP* and the 1789 *BCP* to the 1764 *Scottish Communion Office* and to the 1662 *BCP*. Even as the first bishops of the American Episcopal Church were consecrated by both Scottish and English Bishops in the 1780s, so the first official American Prayer Book traced its content to both the English and Scottish Prayer Books.

From the ancient Church via Scotland

Samuel Seabury of the diocese of Connecticut was consecrated at Aberdeen in Scotland by three Scottish Episcopal bishops on November 14, 1784. The next day he signed a "Concordat or Bond of Union between the Catholic remainder of the ancient Church of Scotland and the now rising Church in the State of Connecticut." The fifth of the seven articles of this document required Seabury to do all within his power to ensure that the Rite for Holy Communion in his State follow that of the Scottish Episcopal Church of 1764. He was "to make the Celebration of this venerable Mystery conformable to the most primitive Doctrine and Practice," and thereby return to the principles of the first Prayer Book of the Anglican Way, that of 1549.

Seabury kept his promise and a slightly modified form of the Scottish Office was used in his diocese not only until the arrival of the new American Prayer Book of 1789 but in some parishes into the nineteenth century. Thus the diocese of Connecticut was not present in the Fall of 1785 at the Philadelphia Convention of Anglicans from other States when a revised 1662 *BCP* was proposed and printed in order to be submitted to the Archbishop of Canterbury, along with the request that two American priests be consecrated bishops for the growing and now independent American Episcopal Church. The proposed 1785 Book was rejected by Canterbury but eventually the priests, William White and Samuel Provoost, were ordained and consecrated in Lambeth Palace on February 4, 1787.

Writing to Bishop White on June 29,1789, Seabury explained his reservations concerning the Order for Holy Communion in the 1662 Book.

> The grand fault in that office is the deficiency of a more formal oblation of the elements, and of the invocation of the Holy Ghost to sanctify and bless them. The Consecration is made to consist merely in the Priest's laying his hands on the elements and pronouncing *This is my body &c.*, which words are not consecration at all, nor were they addressed by Christ to the Father, but were declarative to the Apostles. This is so exactly symbolizing with the Church of Rome in an error; an error, too, on which the absurdity of Transubstantiation is built, that nothing but having fallen into the same error themselves, could have prevented the enemies of the Church from casting in her teeth. The efficacy of Baptism, of Confirmation, of Orders, is ascribed to the Holy Ghost, and His energy is implored for that purpose; and why should He not be invoked in the consecration of the Eucharist, especially as all the old Liturgies are full to the point, I cannot conceive.

And looking forward to the Convention, soon to meet, Seabury went on to say:

> I hope it [the revision of the Eucharistic Prayer in the 1662 Book] will be taken up, and that God will raise up

some able and worthy advocate for this primitive practice, and make you and the Convention the instruments
of restoring it to His Church in America. It would do you
more honour in the world, and contribute more to the union
of the churches than any other alterations you can make,
and would restore the Holy Eucharist to its ancient dig-
nity and efficacy (Bishop William White, *Memoirs of the
Church*, 1830, pp.154-155).

The thinking of Seabury is significant. For him, as for the
Nonjurors and the Scottish Episcopalians, the Anglican
Church is not to imitate the Roman Church: rather it is to
look for authenticity for the Eucharist to the ancient Liturgies from the period when the Church produced her great
doctrinal statements in the Councils of Nicea (325) and
Constantinople (381). In fact he is committed to a development of doctrine from that of the 1662 Book with regard to
the Eucharist, and he is desirous to see this development
shared by the whole Episcopal Church in America.

On October 14, 1789, both Houses of the Convention
agreed to the new Prayer Book, whose Eucharistic Prayer
followed closely that of the Scottish model. A successor of
Seabury as Bishop of Connecticut commented: "Scotland
gave us [the American Church] a greater boon than when
she gave us the Episcopate," adding that (as events turned
out and showed) the Episcopate could have been obtained
solely from England, but England could not have given to
America an authentic Eucharistic Prayer. Only Scotland
could have given that, and, by the providence of God, through
Seabury having to seek consecration in Scotland after fail-
ing in England, Scotland had actually given that Prayer to
American Anglicanism (*The American Church Review*, 1882).

Though Seabury was able to get the adoption of the Scottish Eucharistic Prayer with the help of White by the Convention, this did not mean that the clergy of the Middle
States and Southern States shared his theological opinion
of its necessity so as to have a truly valid Communion Rite.
The same Convention refused to allow the Athanasian Creed
into the Prayer Book, even though Bishop White supported
Seabury in this move. White was much more representa-

tive of American Episcopalianism than was Seabury, and of White one who knew him well wrote:

> Bishop White's theological opinions... were decidely Anti-Calvinistic, and may be classed with what was currently denominated "Arminianism" in the last century. He was, to the last, opposed to the theory comprised in the words *Priest, Altar, Sacrifice*, this being one of the few points on which he was highly sensitive. The good Bishop's ecclesiastical views were those known in history as Low-church. It was not the Low-churchmanship of the present day [i.e., evangelical] but that of [the English Latitudinarians] Tillotson, Burnet and that portion of the English Divines with which they were associated. (Henry U. Onderdonk on William White in Wm B.Sprague, *Annals of the American Episcopal Pulpit*, New York, 1859, pp.284-5.)

In other words, the mindset of White was that of an eighteenth-century Latitudinarian; He was a genial, intelligent, devout and broad-minded man, who came in his later years to dislike the growing enthusiasm of the evangelicals and to appreciate the urbane high churchmanship of Bishop Hobart of New York.

The Content of the 1928 Order for Communion

The first official Prayer Book of the now independent American Protestant Episcopal Church became that of 1789, not the Latitudinarian "Proposed Book" of 1785. To it was added an Ordinal in 1792 and the *Thirty-Nine Articles* in 1801. A revision of the Prayer Book and Ordinal was completed in 1892 and a further one in 1928. The latter revision included a petition for the departed and some changes in order following the order of the Scottish 1637 Prayer Book. These caused great controversy at the time, even as did similar proposals in England. In fact, it is significant that the 1928 *BCP* was produced at the same time as prayer-book revision was proceeding in various parts of the Anglican Communion, and chiefly in England. While the London Parliament blocked the adoption of the new 1928 English

Book, the American Church, free of all State control, authorized the use of its own, and the 1928 *BCP* remained the Prayer Book of the Episcopal Church of the USA until, regrettably, it placed the 1928 *BCP* in its archives and adopted the very different type of Prayer Book in 1979 (see chapters 10 & 11).

The contents of the 1928 Order of Holy Communion are as follows:

The Lord's Prayer
The Collect for Purity
The Commandments
The *Kyrie*
The Collect
The Collect of the Day
The Epistle
(*An anthem or hymn*)
The Gospel
The Creed
The Offertory
The Prayer for the Whole State of Christ's Church
"Ye that do truly..."
The Absolution
The Comfortable Words
Sursum Corda
The Proper Preface
Sanctus
The Eucharistic Prayer
    The Consecration
    The Oblation
    The Invocation
The Lord's Prayer
"We do not presume..."
Administration of Holy Communion
Prayer of Thanksgiving
Gloria in Excelsis
The Blessing

Unlike the 1662 Book, the Exhortations are printed at the end of the Service and, when used, are to be said, after the prayer for the whole state of Christ's Church.

Significantly, a rubric directs that, after the offerings of the people have been received, "the Priest shall then offer, and shall place upon the Holy Table, the Bread and the Wine." The key word is *offer* and recalls the words of the 1637 Scottish *BCP* - "the Presbyter shall offer up and place the bread and wine prepared for the Sacrament upon the Lord's Table."

There are no directions concerning the Mixed Chalice in this Rite. Further, there are no directions concerning the Lavabo, or the ceremonial washing of the hands of the celebrant, after the preparation of the Table. The absence of directions presumably implies that these actions are optional. As we have noted the Mixed Chalice was seen as very important by those who also wished to conform the Eucharistic Prayer to the patristic models.

The Eucharistic Prayer

	Lift up your hearts.
Answer.	**We lift them up unto the Lord.**
Priest.	**Let us give thanks unto our Lord God.**
Answer.	**It is meet and right so to do.**

Then shall the Priest turn to the Holy Table, and say,

It is very meet, right, and our bounden duty, that we should at all times, and in all places, give thanks unto thee, O Lord, Holy Father, Almighty, Everlasting God.

Here shall follow the Proper Preface, according to the time, if there be any specially appointed; or else immediately shall be said or sung by the Priest,

THEREFORE with Angels and Archangels, and with all the company of heaven, we laud and magnify thy glorious Name; evermore praising thee, and saying,

Priest and People.

HOLY, HOLY, HOLY, Lord God of hosts, Heaven and earth are full of thy glory: Glory be to thee, O Lord Most High. Amen.

When the Priest, standing before the Holy Table, hath so ordered the Bread and Wine, that he may with the more readiness and decency break the Bread before the People, and take the Cup into his hands, he shall say the Prayer of Consecration, as followeth.

ALL glory be to thee, Almighty God, our heavenly Father, for that thou, of thy tender mercy, didst give thine only Son Jesus Christ to suffer death upon the Cross for our redemption; who made there (by his one oblation of himself once offered) a full, perfect, and sufficient sacrifice, oblation, and satisfaction, for the sins of the whole world; and did institute, and in his holy Gospel command us to continue, a perpetual memory of that his precious death and sacrifice, until his coming again: For in the night in which he was betrayed, (a) he took Bread; and when he had given thanks, (b) he brake it, and gave it to his disciples, saying, Take, eat, (c) this is my Body, which is given for you; Do this in remembrance of me. Likewise, after supper, (d) he took the Cup; and when he had given thanks, he gave it to them, saying, Drink ye all of this; for (e) this is my Blood of the New Testament, which is shed for you, and for many, for the remission of sins; Do this, as oft as ye shall drink it, in remembrance of me.

[Manual acts are required at a,b,c,d, & e.]

The Oblation

WHEREFORE, O Lord and heavenly Father, according to the institution of thy dearly beloved Son our Saviour Jesus Christ, we, thy humble servants, do celebrate and make here before thy Divine Majesty, with these thy holy gifts, which we now offer unto thee, the memorial thy Son hath commanded us to make; having in remembrance his blessed passion and precious death, his mighty resurrection and glorious ascension; rendering unto thee most hearty thanks for the innumerable benefits procured unto us by the same.

The Invocation.

AND we most humbly beseech thee, O merciful Father, to hear us; and, of thy almighty goodness, vouchsafe to bless and sanctify, with thy Word and Holy Spirit, these thy gifts and creatures of bread and wine; that we, receiving them according to thy Son our Saviour Jesus Christ's holy institution, in remembrance of his death and passion, may be partakers of his most blessed Body and Blood.

AND we earnestly desire thy fatherly goodness, mercifully to accept this our sacrifice of praise and thanksgiving; most humbly beseeching thee to grant that, by the merits and death of thy Son Jesus Christ, and through faith in his blood, we, and all thy whole Church, may obtain remission of our sins, and all other benefits of his passion. And here we offer and present unto thee, O Lord, ourselves, our souls and bodies, to be a reasonable, holy, and living sacrifice unto thee; humbly beseeching thee, that we, and all others who shall be partakers of this Holy Communion, may worthily receive the most precious Body and Blood of thy Son Jesus Christ, be filled with thy grace and heavenly benediction, and made one body with him, that he may dwell in us, and we in him. And although we are unworthy, through our manifold sins, to offer unto thee any sacrifice; yet we beseech thee to accept this our bounden duty and service; not weighing our merits, but pardoning our offences, through Jesus Christ our Lord; by whom, and with whom, in the unity of the Holy Ghost, all honour and glory be unto thee, O Father Almighty, world without end. *Amen.*

And now, as our Saviour Christ hath taught us, we are bold to say,

OUR Father, who art in heaven, Hallowed be thy Name.
Thy kingdom come. Thy will be done, On earth as it is in
heaven. Give us this day our daily bread. And forgive us
our trespasses, As we forgive those who trespass against
us. And lead us not into temptation, But deliver us from
evil. For thine is the kingdom, and the power, and the glory,
for ever and ever. Amen.

*Then shall the Priest, kneeling down at the Lord's Table, say, in
the name of all those who shall receive the Communion, this Prayer
following.*

WE do not presume to come to this thy Table, O merciful
Lord, trusting in our own righteousness, but in thy manifold and great mercies. We are not worthy so much as to
gather up the crumbs under thy Table. But thou art the
same Lord, whose property is always to have mercy: Grant
us therefore, gracious Lord, so to eat the flesh of thy dear
Son Jesus Christ, and to drink his blood, that our sinful
bodies may be made clean by his body, and our souls washed
through his most precious blood, and that we may evermore dwell in him, and he in us. *Amen.*

Here may be sung a Hymn.

*Then shall the Priest first receive the Holy Communion in both
kinds himself, and proceed to deliver the same to the Bishops,
Priests, and Deacons, in like manner, (if any be present,) and, after
that, to the People also in order, into their hands, all devoutly
kneeling. And sufficient opportunity shall be given to those present
to communicate. And when he delivereth the Bread, he shall say,*

THE Body of our Lord Jesus Christ, which was given for
thee, preserve thy body and soul unto everlasting life. Take
and eat this in remembrance that Christ died for thee, and
feed on him in thy heart by faith, with thanksgiving.

And the Minister who delivereth the Cup shall say,

THE Blood of our Lord Jesus Christ, which was shed for thee, preserve thy body and soul unto everlasting life. Drink this in remembrance that Christ's Blood was shed for thee, and be thankful.

If the consecrated Bread or Wine be spent before all have communicated, the Priest is to consecrate more, according to the Form before prescribed; beginning at, All glory be to thee, Almighty God, *and ending with these words,* partakers of his most blessed Body and Blood.

When all have communicated, the Priest shall return to the Lord's Table, and reverently place upon it what remaineth of the consecrated Elements, covering the same with a fair linen cloth.

Then shall the Priest say,

Let us pray.

ALMIGHTY and everliving God, we most heartily thank thee, for that thou dost vouchsafe to feed us who have duly received these holy mysteries, with the spiritual food of the most precious Body and Blood of thy Son our Saviour Jesus Christ; and dost assure us thereby of thy favour and goodness towards us; and that we are very members incorporate in the mystical body of thy Son, which is the blessed company of all faithful people; and are also heirs through hope of thy everlasting kingdom, by the merits of his most precious death and passion. And we humbly beseech thee, O heavenly Father, so to assist us with thy grace, that we may continue in that holy fellowship, and do all such good works as thou hast prepared for us to walk in; through Jesus Christ our Lord, to whom, with thee and the Holy Ghost, be all honour and glory, world without end. *Amen.*

Then shall be said the Gloria in excelsis, all standing, or some proper Hymn.

Reflections

The text of the 1928 Rite, as it stands and without additions from the Missal (which coming from the Roman Rite do not fit so well into a Rite which is imitating Eastern Rites - see chapter nine), is the kind of text for which the classical Anglicans (or Caroline Divines) of the early seventeenth century, the Nonjurors, some English theologians of the High Church School and the Scottish Episcopal Church of the seventeenth and eighteenth century worked and prayed.

It is a Service, which on its own terms and according to its own logic and rubrics, is a fine example of a Rite that seeks to follow the principles of One Scripture, Two Testaments. Four Councils and Five Centuries (see chapter two). It does not, of course, follow the principle of the Three Creeds, because there is no place for the Athanasian Creed in the 1928 *BCP*, though the Nicene Creed does contain the *filioque* ("and from the Son") of the Western Church, and the Preface and Collect for Trinity Sunday are expressions of the Western dogma of the Trinity.

It seems to me regrettable that the way of celebration of this Rite is so often today with additions from the Missal and thus from the Gregorian Canon or Roman Rite. Thus, it is being made to conform to the pre-Vatican II Roman Canon. Those who pioneered the development of the 1637 and 1764 Rites as well as the Nonjurors, who produced their own Rites, were in certain ways anti-Roman. They wished to develop the Communion Service in ways, which were dependent on Eastern Rites, that are more ancient than, and somewhat different from, the Western Rites. Therefore, it is not surprising that the Antiochene Orthodox Church permits as a Western Rite within its jurisdiction a slightly adapted form of the 1928 Rite.

My conclusion is clear. The 1928 *Order for Holy Communion* is a right Rite for today and is an excellent Rite for those on the Canterbury or the Liturgical trail, who are desirous to recover the essence and ethos of patristic religion for the modern American scene. While the 1662 is the best for those who are wanting to be evangelically reformed catholic and western, the 1928 is the best for those who want to have a practical sense of unity with the Church which produced the Niceno-Constantinopolitan Creed (325 & 381) and the Eastern Liturgies.

CHAPTER EIGHT

The REC Book of 1874

We noted in the last chapter that at a Convention of the Protestant Episcopal Church held at Philadelphia from September 27 to October 7, 1785, a revised *Book of Common Prayer* was proposed. It was a revision of the 1662 *BCP* in what we could call today a Liberal direction. Though it never became the official Prayer Book of the Episcopal Church, it did become, after some revision, the Prayer Book of the Reformed Episcopal Church from 1873.

Before 1785 the Episcopal Church had been using, because of the historic and legal connexion with the Church of England, the 1662 *BCP*, and thus this was the Book that was set to be revised for the future use of the Protestant Episcopal Church as an independent Church. So it was the 1785 revision of the 1662 *BCP* that was sent to England along with the appeal for the ordaining and consecration of American priests as bishops for the American Church. However, the Archbishop of Canterbury was not pleased with the revised 1785 proposed *BCP* and would not accept it!

The Latitudinarian and Evangelical Context

Since the general climate of thought at the end of the eighteenth century was still tending towards Unitarianism, Deism and Latitudinarianism, it is not surprising that the revisions made to the 1662 text in Philadelphia were away from classical orthodoxy and towards a less doctrinally dogmatic religion. The Athanasian Creed with its clear teaching on the Holy Trinity and the Person of Christ was removed. The initial Lord's Prayer and the Nicene Creed were both dropped from the Communion Service. This was based on the assumption that the Lord's Prayer had already been said, and the Apostles' Creed recited, at Morning Prayer which normally preceded the Order for the Administration of the Lord's Supper. (At that time the "metaphysical" nature of the Nicene Creed's description of Jesus Christ was out of favor. Thus, no Nicene Creed. Further, the Apostles' Creed was printed without the words, "he descended into hell," since this was regarded as merely stating that he descended into the grave.) Also, the *Gloria in Excelsis* was abbreviated in the second paragraph, and the Black Rubric concerning kneeling was deleted.

Since this proposed Prayer Book of 1785 never became the official *Book of Common Prayer* of the Protestant Episcopal Church (later the Episcopal Church of the United States of America - ECUSA) its history should have ended in 1786 when revision of it occurred at the Convention. Further, it should have ended in 1789, when the Church had its own Bishops, and a different Book, which included the Nicene Creed and which markedly showed the influence of the *Scottish Communion Office* on the Eucharistic Prayer. Instead, the 1785 text lay sleeping for nearly a century before it was revived for use by the new Reformed Episcopal Church in 1873.

In a certificate in the reprint of the 1785 Book, Bishop George David Cummins, founding Bishop of the Reformed Episcopal Church and former Bishop of the Protestant Episcopal Church, wrote on December 8, 1873 as follows:

> I hereby certify that this Prayer-Book, now reissued by the Reformed Episcopal Church is - with the exception of the omitted portions, namely, the Visitation Office, the Proposed Articles of Religion, in which the original number was reduced to twenty, and the metrical Psalms - an exact reprint of the English edition of 1785. It will subjected to revision before being finally set forth for general use.

The nature of the future revision was to be according to the *Declaration of Principles* adopted by the General Council of the new denomination on December 2, 1873. The Visitation of the Sick was omitted because it contained an absolution given by the priest, a practice rejected by Cummins and his new church.

The *Declaration of Principles* represents an attempt to be committed to Anglican evangelicalism, to oppose Anglo-Catholicism, and to have fellowship with Evangelicals in the other main-line Protestant denominations. The substance of the *Declaration* was not a new idea in 1873 for it had been set forth by the well-known William Augustus Muhlenberg in 1854 in his attempts to promote evangelical unity. As the *Principles* have remained central to the theology and liturgy of the Reformed Episcopal Church; and are required by Article IX of the REC's, *Constitution and Canons*, to be printed in the front of every official publication of the church, it is necessary to state them in full:

I

The Reformed Episcopal Church, holding "the faith once delivered unto the saints," declares its belief in the Holy Scriptures of the Old and New Testaments as the Word of God, and the sole Rule of Faith and Practice; in the Creed "commonly called the Apostles' Creed;" in the Divine institution of the Sacraments of Baptism and the Lord's Supper; and in the doctrines of grace substantially as they are set forth in the Thirty-Nine Articles of Religion.

II

This Church recognizes and adheres to Episcopacy, not as of Divine right, but as a very ancient and desirable form of Church polity.

III

This Church, retaining a Liturgy which shall not be imperative or repressive of freedom in prayer, accepts *The Book of Common Prayer* as it was revised, proposed and recommended for use by the General Convention of the Protestant Episcopal Church, A.D. 1785, reserving full liberty to alter, abridge, enlarge, and amend the same, as may seem most conducive to the edification of the people, "provided that the substance of the faith be kept entire."

IV

This Church condemns and rejects the following erroneous and strange doctrines as contrary to God's Word:

First, That the Church of Christ exists only in one order or form of ecclesiastical polity:

Second, That Christian Ministers are "priests" in another sense than that in which all believers are "a royal priesthood:"

Third, That the Lord's Table is an altar on which the oblation of the Body and Blood of Christ is offered anew to the Father:

Fourth, That the Presence of Christ in the Lord's Supper is a presence in the elements of Bread and Wine:

Fifth, That Regeneration is inseparably connected with Baptism.

It will be observed that there is no mention of the Nicene Creed. Further, the commitment to the Thirty-Nine Articles could be read as incomplete, being only to the doctrine of grace taught by them. However, if the meaning of the first principle is a total commitment to the Thirty-Nine Articles, then actions taken later by the Reformed Episcopal Church are actually in opposition to this *Declaration,* which according to the "Constitution and Canons" is "unalterable."

The attachment to Episcopacy is that of seeing the Historic Episcopate not as of the *esse* (the necessary being) or the *plene esse* (the fullness of being) of the Church, but only - at best - as of the *bene esse* (the well being) of the Church. It is desirable but not absolutely necessary. Thus the Reformed Episcopal Church has neither re-ordained nor even conditionally ordained "Ministers" entering its Ministry from other denominations. Finally, the rejection of the Anglo-Catholic movement and its theology is abundantly evident in the statements about the Sacraments.

The Prayer Book of 1874

If we now turn to *The Book of Common Prayer* of the Reformed Episcopal Church, which was adopted and set forth for use by the General Council of the Church at New York in May 1874, we get a good understanding of where this new evangelical denomination was going theologically and liturgically. Its Preface, like that of the 1785 Book, appeals to and praises the attempt made in England in 1689, on the accession of William and Mary, to revise the Liturgy, Articles of Religion, and Canons of the Church of England to allow for a greater latitude of interpretation of the Church's teaching and to make possible the re-entry of those who were then being called Protestant Dissenters or Nonconformists. Further, it sees the revision of the 1662 *BCP* in the 1785 Book as being the continuation of the good work of 1689.

However, since the Protestant Episcopal Church never followed through with that "good work" but adopted an "unrevised Prayer Book" in 1789, now the Reformed Episcopal Church has done what ought to have been done in 1689 and 1785! Apparently Bishop Cummins and his colleagues were not fully aware that the inspiration for the 1689 revision was partly, and, for the 1785 revision, was nearly wholly, liberal or Latitudinarian in motivation and purpose.

After the Preface and the "Declaration of Principles" (quoted above), the new Thirty-Five Articles are printed. These reveal clearly that the new Church is intent on being a decidedly *evangelical* Church; defining *evangelical* in late nineteenth-century terms, and in the context of a sense of doing battle with Anglo-Catholics and Roman Catholics in order to preserve the truth of the Gospel. It is not certain whether these Articles were adopted by the General Council in addition to, or in place of the Thirty-Nine Articles. However, it is the case that these new Articles have been printed at the front of every Prayer Book since 1874. The Thirty-Five cannot by any reasonable judgment be said to be Anglican.

Certainly the original Thirty-Nine posed difficulties in that they regularly used the word "priest" for the minister (Articles XXXI, XXXII, and XXXVI) and also there is in them one article (Article III) on "The going down of Christ into hell", which hardly agreed with the version of the Apostles' Creed in the 1785 proposed Book and the actual 1874 Book, used in the Reformed Episcopal Church.

However, since evangelicals were generally ready to use the Nicene Creed, this Creed returns to the 1874 Prayer Book along with the Apostles' Creed (without the "he descended into hell") both in the Daily Offices and in the Order for the Administration of the Lord's Supper.

A perusal of the "The Form of Ordaining Deacons" and "The Form of Ordaining Presbyters" [the word "priest" is not used of ministers] and "The Form of Consecrating a Bishop" in the 1874 Book provides a clear view of the understanding of what the leaders of the new church believed is the ordained ministry. A clear distinction is made between the Deacon and the Presbyter, but the Bishop (who is never addressed as "Reverend Father in God" as in the 1662 Book) is viewed as a Presbyter who has been elevated to a position of superintendency or as senior shepherd.

This interpretation is suggested by two facts. *First,* the service is called "The Form of Consecrating a Bishop" whereas the 1662 Ordinal has "The Form of Ordaining and Consecrating a bishop," in order to make clear that the Episcopate is a different office and order to that of the presbyterate or ministerial priesthood. *In the second place,* the 1874 Service requires that not only the officiating bishop along with any other bishops present, but also three or more presbyters lay their hands upon the head of the presbyter being consecrated bishop. The function of "consecration" thus appears to be that of "being set apart for a particular office within the order of presbyters." The REC, however, claims to have bishops in the full Anglican sense. This said, the office of Bishop in the REC is for life, and there is "functionally" a House of Bishops in the organization of the Reformed Episcopal Church.

In the ordination of the Presbyter there is no reference whatsoever to the authority to absolve repentant sinners.

In the 1662 Service are the words: "Receive the Holy Ghost for the office and work of a Priest in the Church of God, now committed unto thee by the imposition of our hands. Whose sins thou dost forgive, they are forgiven; and whose sins thou dost retain are retained..." The fact that this is missing in the 1874 Book is in total harmony with the fact that there is in the 1874 Book neither any Absolution in Holy Communion nor in the Visitation of the Sick. Further, the apparent Absolution or Declaration of Forgiveness in the Daily Office is in fact a prayer for God to forgive.

Since the Presbyter and the Bishop cannot give Absolution but may simply declare it on the basis of Scripture promises (as any layperson can do) then this has the effect of making the Lord's Supper more like that of the Presbyterians or Methodists in doctrinal and spiritual content.

The contents of the REC Order for the Lord's Supper are as follows:

A Hymn
"The Lord be with you"
The Versicles
The Lord's Prayer
The Collect for Purity
The Ten Commandments and the Summary of the Law
A Prayer for Grace to keep the Law
The Collect of the Day
The Epistle
The Gospel
The Apostles' or Nicene Creed [*At the end of the Nicene creed there is a Note stating that by "One Catholic and Apostolic Church" is signified "The blessed company of all faithful people;" and by "One Baptism for the remission of sins" the Baptism of the Holy Ghost.*]
A Hymn
The Sermon
An Invitation [*Our fellow Christians of other branches of Christ's Church, and all who love our Divine Lord and Savior Jesus Christ in sincerity, are affectionately invited to the Lord's Table.*]
Scriptural Sentences and Collection of Money
The Prayer for the whole state of Christ's Church militant

The Exhortation
"Ye that do truly and earnestly..."
The Confession of Sins
A Declaration of Forgiveness (optional)
The Comfortable Words
The *Sursum Corda*
The Proper Preface when required
The *Sanctus*
"We do not presume..."
The Prayer of Consecration
A Hymn
The Administration of Communion
The *Gloria in Excelsis*
The Prayer of Thanksgiving
The Blessing (Dismissal)

The Prayer of Consecration is essentially that of 1662 except that there are no required manual acts of taking the Paten and the Cup by the Minister in his hands. Further, the Proper Prefaces are not all those of 1662 or of 1785. Most were rewritten to simplify the classical Trinitarian doctrine; in the event they end up virtually rejecting classical, western Trinitarianism.

One of the rubrics requires that "in conducting this Service, except when kneeling, the Minister shall face the people." This is intended to exclude any possibility of Eastward celebration. Since the "Consecration Prayer" is a prayer, the minister was to kneel at the North end of the Table, as had been the custom before 1789 in America and up to the influence of the Anglo-Catholic movement in England. At the Administration it is assumed that the people are "around the Table," which is to be away from the wall.

Further the Administration is different from that of 1662 and 1785. The Minister says the words "The Body...everlasting life" to all the Communicants around the Table, and then to each one as he delivers the Bread he says, "Take and eat *this bread* in remembrance..." Likewise in delivering the Cup the Minister addresses all in saying, "The Blood...everlasting life," and then to each one as he delivers the Cup he says "Drink *this wine* in remembrance..." Obviously, the insertion of the words "bread" and "wine" was intended to remove any possible understanding of the consecrated elements in terms of a Presence in, with, under, around or through them.

A final Note picks up the content of the old Black Rubric from 1552 and 1662 in stating: "The act and prayer of consecration do not change the nature of the elements, but merely set them apart for holy use; and the reception of them in a kneeling posture is not an act of adoration of the elements."

There is no provision in the 1874 Book (in contrast to the 1662 and 1785 Books) for any further consecration if the Minister uses that which he has placed on the Table before he has given Communion to all present. This omission takes us back to the 1552 *BCP* and suggests a rejection of the Anglican tradition since the late sixteenth century.

Further revisions of the 1874 Book

The 1874 Prayer Book has been revised four times - 1882, 1894, 1896 and 1963. The fifth edition, which is still in use in 1994, contains the Thirty-Five Articles and prints on the last page of the introductory material (p.xxx) the following extract from the Constitution (Article VIII):

> Nothing calculated to teach, either directly or symbolically, that the Christian Ministry possesses a sacerdotal character, or that the Lord's Supper is a sacrifice, shall ever be allowed in the worship of this Church; nor shall any communion table be constructed in the form of an altar.
>
> No retable shall be erected in any church, and no candle, candlestick or cross shall be placed upon the Communion Table. The table shall be so placed that the Minister may stand behind it.

A "retable" is a shelf behind the "altar" or "table" on which may be placed a cross, candlesticks or other objects. It is also called a "gradine."

In the Order for Holy Communion there are a few changes from 1874. For example, the Declaration of Forgiveness after the Confession of Sins is removed so that there is no

Absolution or Declaration of Forgiveness; the Proper Preface for Trinity Sunday is restored to the 1662 form of words; the order of prayers after the administration of Communion is changed so that the *Gloria in Excelsis* is made to follow the Prayer of Thanksgiving (which is now a choice from three prayers), rather than to precede it.

Conclusion

In recent decades a significant minority within the Reformed Episcopal Church has called for a return to where it is believed the founder, Bishop Cummins, wanted the Church to go. That is, to seek to become a decidedly evangelical expression of Anglicanism using the 1662 *BCP* and *Ordinal*, suitably adapted to American conditions, and guided doctrinally by the original *Thirty-Nine Articles*. To do this will mean not only shedding the 1874 Prayer Book and its successors but also rejecting the Thirty-Five Articles and rewriting the Canons. If the Church has to keep its "unalterable" *Declaration of Principles* then it can easily use the word "presbyter" as did the Scottish Prayer Books of 1637 and 1764.

It is my conviction, as a friend of the Church, that the right Rite for the Reformed Episcopal Church is undoubtedly the full 1662 Rite along with the whole of the 1662 *BCP* used and celebrated by Bishops, Presbyters and Deacons, who are themselves ordained according to the 1662 Ordinal! Whether these services are available in only traditional English form or also in modern English is, I think, a secondary matter. The main point is the actual use of the 1662 Book with its reformed catholic theology.

The sister Churches of the Reformed Episcopal Church in Canada, England, and South Africa use a revised 1662 *BCP*. Thus, it seems appropriate for the whole family to conform to the 1662 pattern. In the American context, however, where every denomination needs to have its distinctives, the Reformed Episcopal Church can stand (without any competitors!) on and for the 1662 *BCP*. Thereby, it will be distinguished from, but related to, other branches of the Anglican family.

CHAPTER NINE

A Missal for Anglicans

The Missal is the traditional word for the altar book, the large book containing the texts needed to celebrate the Eucharist. Before the arrival of the 1549 *Book of Common Prayer* the Missal on the altar was the norm for celebration of the Mass in cathedrals and parish churches. One of the developments within the Anglo-Catholic movement was the felt need (especially in religious orders) for a Missal, which made provision for the daily celebration of the Mass; and did so in a way which declared both that the Anglican Rite is only a variation of the classic Roman Rite, and that the Anglican Rite needs supplementing from the Roman Rite.

There are two Anglican Missals in use today. One is known as *The American Missal* (1931, rev.ed.,1951) and the other as *The Anglican Missal in the American Edition* (1943, rev.ed.,1947). Though they are used (relatively speaking) in only a small number of parishes within the Episcopal Church and the Continuing Churches, the general influence of the ceremonial and prayers of the Missals is more broadly spread. This influence is seen both in words and in actions. For example, the addition of the personal prayer (known as the *Domine, non sum dignus*), by the priest at Communion - "Lord I am not worthy: that thou shouldest come under my roof: but speak the word only and my soul shall be healed." And the addition of such ceremonial actions as the elevation of the Host and the Chalice with genuflections during the Prayer of Consecration.

In an effort to be a meaningful part of the ECUSA and use the 1979 Episcopal Book in the spirit of the Missal, one group of Anglo-Catholics at Rosemont in Pennsylvania produced in 1991 what they called *The Anglican Service Book: A Traditional Language Adaptation of the 1979 BCP with the Psalter or Psalms of David and Additional Devotions.* This Book has helped conservative Anglo-Catholics live with the modern liturgy. However, it is doubtful whether the Rite in this service book is as genuinely Trinitarian and Christological in an orthodox sense as the old Gregorian/Roman Rite actually is. (See further the comments in chapter eleven concerning the improvement of the 1979 Rite in terms of classic orthodoxy).

The American Missal

In the preface to the *American Missal* of 1951, the editor Earle Hewitt Maddux, S.S.J.E., wrote this:

> The Episcopal Church in this country is part of the ancient Catholic Church in communion with the see of Canterbury. Most of the material contained in this Missal is part of our heritage as members of that historic Church. In producing this book, "We have restored our own ancient customs and usages, or established such new ones as are suited to our needs." These words, written by Saint Gregory the Great to John of Syracuse some fourteen centuries ago, are equally expressive for our own time and the present occasion.

In other words, the Missal looks back through the Reformation to Western Catholic Christianity in England, in Western Europe and in Rome. The structure, content and ceremonial of the Roman Rite fills out the Rite of the *Book of Common Prayer.*

Looking through the contents of this Missal, it is clear that what is being presented is an Anglican Way of being [Roman] western Catholic. That is, there is an imitating of the traditional Roman Missal [pre-Vatican II] but without the legal and canonical relation to the Roman Catholic hierarchy.

The greater part of the Missal is taken up with the Propers of the Seasons (Introit, Collect, Lesson, Gospel, Offertory sentences, Secret Prayer, Postcommunion Prayer). Then there is the printing both of the text of the 1928 Rite without additions and "The Ordinary and Canon of the Mass," which is the 1928 Rite set within the general framework and content of the Roman Rite, but with the 1928 Canon or Eucharistic Prayer.

The Ordinary begins with the preparation by the priest, with deacon, sub-deacon and server, before the lowest altar step. Here there is confession of sins and absolution, with the recital of Psalm 43 and versicles. Then as a sung mass begins there is the blessing of incense and the censing of the altar. In fact, all throughout the Rite there is an abundance of specific instructions as to the posture, deportment and actions of the priest and concerning the use of incense.

At the Offertory the priest offers the Paten with the bread, praying the *Suscipe, sancte Pater*:

Receive, O holy Father, Almighty, Everlasting God, this spotless Host, which I, thine unworthy servant, do offer unto thee, my God, the living and the true, for my countless sins, offences, and negligences, for all here present, and for all the faithful in Christ, both quick and dead: that it may be profitable both to me and to them for salvation unto life eternal. Amen.

Also, after a prayer at the pouring of a drop of water into the wine in the Chalice, the priest offers the Mixed Chalice, praying:

We offer unto thee, O Lord, the cup of salvation, humbly beseeching thy mercy, that it may go up before thy Divine Majesty with a sweet savour for our salvation, and for that of the whole world. Amen.

After placing the Chalice behind the Paten on the Altar he prays:

In the spirit of humility and with a contrite heart, let us be accepted by thee, O Lord; and so let our sacrifice be in thy sight this day, that it may be well pleasing unto thee, O Lord our God.

Then the priest asks for the descent of the Holy Spirit:

Come, O Sanctifier, Almighty, Everlasting God, and bless this Sacrifice prepared for thy holy Name.

Following censing of the Altar and the Lavabo (the ceremonial washing of the hands while saying Psalm 26:6-12) he prays:

Receive, O Holy Trinity, this Oblation which we offer unto thee in memory of the Passion, Resurrection, and Ascension of Jesus Christ our Lord; and in honour of the blessed Mary ever Virgin, of blessed John the Baptist, of the holy Apostles Peter and Paul, and of all the Saints: that it may avail them to their honour, and us to our salvation; and may they whose memory we celebrate on earth vouchsafe to intercede for us in heaven; through the same Christ our Lord. Amen.

Finally, before beginning the prayer for the whole state of Christ's Church, the priest kisses the altar and says:

Pray, brethren, that my sacrifice and yours may be acceptable to God the Father Almighty.

May the Lord receive this sacrifice at my hands, to the praise and glory of his Name, to our benefit and to that of all his holy Church. Amen.

All these additions at the Offertory are intended to indicate that the western Catholic doctrine of the Sacrifice of the Mass has been recovered. It is not, however, a repeat of the unique and once-for-all Sacrifice of Calvary, but is the offering of the Memorial of that unique Event.

The actual words of the Eucharistic Prayer or Canon of the Mass are those of the 1928 *BCP* but the plentiful rubrics and instructions for the stance and acts of the priest are from the old Roman Missal - including elevation and genuflections as noted above. After the Eucharistic Prayer there are further additional prayers. One of these is said as a particle of the Host is put into the Chalice:

May this mingling and the consecration of the Body and Blood of our Lord Jesus Christ avail us who partake thereof unto eternal life. Amen.

Then follows the *Agnus Dei* and the "We do not presume...," followed by the Communion of the priest and people.

Here again there are significant additions to the 1928 text. Before receiving the Host with the words from the *BCP*, the priest prays:

I will receive the bread of heaven and call upon the Name of the Lord.

Lord I am not worthy that thou shouldest come under my roof; but speak the word only, and my soul shall be healed.

Before receiving the Chalice (from where he receives also the particle of the Host) the priest says:

What reward shall I give unto the Lord for all the benefits that he hath done unto me? I will receive the cup of salvation and call upon the Name of the Lord, which is worthy to be praised; so shall I be safe from mine enemies.

And then, turning to the people and holding "the Body and Blood of Christ" in view, he says:

Behold the Lamb of God; behold him that taketh away the sins of the world.

Lord, I am not worthy that thou shouldst come under my roof; but speak the word only and my soul shall be healed.

After Communion and during the ablutions, the priest says two prayers, the second being:

Let thy Body, O Lord, which I have taken, and thy Blood which I have drunk, cleave unto my soul; and grant that no spot of sin may remain in me, whom this pure and holy Sacrament hath refreshed; Who livest and reignest, world without end. Amen.

After the post-Communion prayers, the *Gloria in Excelsis* and the Blessing, the Mass ends with the reading of the Prologue of the Gospel of John.

Obviously, this Rite assumes and teaches that Christ is really and truly present in, with and through the actual elements, which are nothing less than his Body and Blood. It is not only that is received by the faithful communicant is the precious Body and Blood, it is also what is on the altar is the precious Body and Blood of Christ. In other words the Roman doctrine of *transubstantiation* is the natural interpretation of the Presence of Christ as implied by this Rite. It will, of course, also allow the Lutheran doctrine of *consubstantiation*. Possibly, some who use it understand the Presence in a *realist* way without any commitment to Aristotelian categories of explanation.

The Anglican Missal

There is a long Introduction to the (English) *Anglican Missal* (American edition, 1947) which goes a long way to help one understand what is both understood by a Missal and what is its purpose. In *The People's Anglican Missal* (reprinted, Athens, Georgia, 1988) there is also an introduction which explains why the "Prayer-Book Rite must be treated as an apocopated liturgy" and supplemented with traditional materials to make a Missal.

The introductions both to the Altar and People's editions state that six types of material have been added, primarily from the Western Rite: (1) Ceremonial directions; (2) Musical notations and helps to good singing and reading; (3) Forms for certain popular liturgical dramas (e.g., the ceremonies of Candlemas, Ash Wednesday, Palm Sunday, Holy Saturday and Easter Eve); (4) Prayers and scriptural lections for many occasions which demand special observance, but for which the Prayer-Book makes no provision; (5) Hymns (i.e., sacred anthems from the Holy Scriptures); and (6) The personal prayers of the celebrant which were all left out of the *BCP* except the Collect for Purity.

There is of course much that is in common between the American and Anglican Missals, although the Anglican Missal has greater choice with respect to the Canon. It prints the whole of the 1549 *BCP* Eucharistic Prayer (which has been used in the Province of the West Indies this century), as well as the 1928 Eucharistic Prayer and the Gregorian Canon (Roman Rite) as translated by Miles Coverdale. With each Canon are instructions for the priest concerning right celebration. It may be claimed that in printing the Roman Canon, which has been used more within Anglican religious orders than parishes, the Missal stepped beyond the limits of Anglican comprehensiveness.

The People's Anglican Missal, which was produced after the altar edition, shows every sign of its editor being deeply influenced by the theory of Gregory Dix (in his *The Shape of the Liturgy*) concerning the fourfold shape of the Eucharist (see further the discussion and critique of this misguided theory in chapter 11). Included in *The People's Anglican Missal,* is a short essay entitled "How to worship at the Eucharist" which sets forth the fourfold action; further the text of the Canon or Eucharistic Prayer is carefully divided into four parts.

In introducing "The Mass of the Faithful" we encounter this explanation of this fourfold shape:

> The Mass is an act of obedience to our Lord who said: DO THIS IN REMEMBRANCE OF ME. The Action is that part of the Mass in which we DO what he DID. We read that he did four things. 1. He took Bread and Wine. 2. He gave thanks. 3. He brake the Bread. 4. He gave it to them. Bear in mind these four acts of The Action.
>
> During the Action the worshipper should obey our Lord by making each one of these acts his own act. (1) *Oblation*. When the Priest takes Bread and Wine and (as the Prayer-Book commands) "offers and places" the same on the Altar, the worshipper should in spirit offer and place himself on the Altar, as an oblation to God, along with that which is there being offered in his name and for his sake. (2) *Consecration*. When the Eucharistic Consecration is said, he should suffer himself to be consecrated in thanksgiving to God along with the oblations. (3) *Utilization*. When the Fracture is made, he should give himself and his will to be broken in sacrifice as God wills; and (4) *Unification*. When the Body of our Lord is given in the Administration of Holy Communion, he should give himself to Christ who thereby gives himself to the worshipper.

Apart from the wisdom of adopting the Dix theory of the fourfold action and imposing it upon Rites which existed before Dix was born, a weakness of this advice is its modern, individualistic flavor, reflecting twentieth-century cultural change. There is no sense here of the priority of the Body of Christ and of the baptized Christian believer as a member of that one Body.

Both Missals assume that worshippers will attend the Mass but not necessarily receive communion - for good reasons. When this situation arises, it is recommended that the worshipper makes an act of spiritual communion saying from the heart a prayer such as the *Anima Christi* - "Soul of Christ, sanctify me. Body of Christ save me..." Further, as with the Roman Missal, both these Missals make provision for Votive Masses. Masses for the Dead, and the Absolution of the Dead.

Reflections

The old Roman Rite is only rarely used in the Roman Catholic Church today. Where there is permission for the pre-Vatican II Mass, then it is used in its original language, but otherwise it is a sacred memory of the past. Thus those Anglican parishes which actually use the Missal in the old Roman way keep alive an important part of the western Christian heritage.

The question as to whether the use of either of the Missals is legitimately Anglican is raised by the content of *The Thirty-Nine Articles of Religion*. I know that some Anglo-Catholics do take the *Articles* seriously, while also using the Missal enthusiastically. I am prepared to believe that they have found a satisfactory way to be Reformed Catholics, holding to what is lasting and true in the Western Catholic tradition while admitting certain insights and doctrinal developments of the Reformation. Their position must involve very fine tuning in the light of the strong words of the *Articles* and the fact that Cranmer left out of the 1549 *BCP* many of the items that have been restored in the Missal.

However, what divided good men in the sixteenth century need not divide today, for living in a highly secularized society causes men to see both the questions and answers concerning the Mass in a different light. Looking back now we see that the Protestant Reformers of the sixteenth century had much more in common with the defenders of Medieval Catholicism than in that in which they differed! For example, both believed wholeheartedly in the Nicene Creed and the Athanasian Creed, and that the Holy Scriptures are the written Word of God.

It must also be borne in mind that, with the massive changes in Roman Catholicism since the Second Vatican Council including the abandonment of the old Liturgy, there is a real, felt need for the full majesty of the traditional western High Mass. If anyone wants that in English then he must go to the traditional Anglo-Catholic parish, which uses the Missal, for the English service he attends at the Roman Catholic parish will not normally use the old Canon in English.

In summary, to use the Missal with spiritual freedom so that the words and the (complex) actions flow together in beauty and harmony only comes to those priests who are both "professional", and prayerful in their celebration. If a priest is overburdened with the seemingly endless instructions and rubrics which he has to follow, and finds that he is in bondage to them, then he ought to use the 1928 Rite according to its own simple rubrics. I fear that in some of the Continuing Anglican Churches priests are being "required" to use the Missal when they have no real taste or empathy with it; therefore, they cannot serve the Lord at the altar with joyful reverence, and the people are thereby not allowed fully to taste and see that the Lord is good. Likewise, I fear that the use of the reprinted *People's Anglican Missal,* without careful instruction concerning its theology and spirituality, is giving a minority of folks an imbalanced sense of what is the Anglican Way.

CHAPTER TEN

Experience Old and New

Since the 1960s the churches of the Anglican Way from Australia to Canada and from England to South Africa have seen the development and adoption of new Prayer Books. In some cases the new Books have replaced the classic *Book of Common Prayer* (as in the American Episcopal Church), and, in other cases, these *Books of Alternative Services* have come alongside as an alternative to the classic Book (as in Canada and England). Regrettably, ecclesiastical authorities have urged and pressured congregations to use the new books first at their best-attended services and then all the time. And seminaries have pushed the new at the expense of the old.

Similar but different

The actual doctrinal content of these new prayer books, when carefully examined, represents a major revision of that found in the traditional Prayer Books. This revision is not always immediately obvious because the traditional "language of Zion" is still used, and further, most worshippers who were brought up in the use of the old book tend to read what they have known into the text of the new book. So differences obvious to the specialist are not usually seen by the average parishioner until they are pointed out and carefully explained.

The fact that there has not been a greater outcry from clergy and laity concerning this revision of doctrine now written into the new liturgies probably is best explained in terms of a changing context. In the universities and seminaries, the older view of doctrine and the pursuit of theology as deduction from Scripture and Tradition, has gradually been giving way to new views which claimed to be in tune with modern ways of academic study and in harmony with the scientific spirit.

In 1970, one of my teachers, the late Professor Ian Ramsey of Oxford University [later Bishop of Durham], claimed that "theology is at present in turmoil...Theology seems often to the outsider just so much word-spinning, air-borne discourse which never touches down except disastrously." (*Models for Divine Activity*, 1973, p.1). In a similar fashion and writing about the same time, Paul L. Holmer, professor of theology at Yale, spoke of the loss of control and authority in theology by such Churches as the Roman Catholic, the Anglican, the Lutheran, and the Reformed or Presbyterian.

> In the name of theology, there is now a vast array of teachings, not quite in agreement with one another, but all of them bidding for attention within these groups. It is very hard, indeed, to make sense of it all. Theology looks almost promiscuous even where confessional views, Biblical allegiance and Christian authority are loudly asserted. For even these time-honored safeguards and criteria have been caught up in the whirl of ideas that counts as theology. (*The Grammar of Faith*, 1978, pp.1-2.)

Anyone who follows the publications of the major denominational presses will know this is still true in the 1990s.

Then, also, major changes had been taking place in the general culture, especially in and from the 1960s. Ordinary parishioners had been gaining a modern "mindset," without perhaps realizing that their thinking patterns were being molded by the powerful winds of modernity. These winds have, at least, conditioned them to turn inwards and look for God more in their present feelings and personal experience than in the transcendent reality of God known in majestic worship or in the discipline of Bible study and meditation.

A major attraction of the modern liturgies has been that they are in a so-called modern English. Gone are all the "thees" and "thous" and all archaic expressions! Folks have accepted the new liturgies solely because they were in a modern form of English, and therefore, seemed to be more useful and acceptable to modern Americans. Strangely, evangelical and charismatic congregations often provide the best examples of this desire to be addressing God in the same way that people address each other today. They tend to see liturgy as a means to an end - e.g., evangelism or church growth or dynamic, spiritual experience - and thus a liturgy in modern English has a greater appeal to them, because it appears to provide fewer barriers in the search for authentic religious experience today. It never seems to occur to them that they would benefit the more by using a classic liturgical text and rendering it into modern English!

If we focus our attention upon the new Prayer Books being used by Episcopalians/Anglicans in North America, we find that there are three we have to consider. In the Episcopal Church (ECUSA) there is *The Book of Common Prayer* (1979) which is now the official book; this is supplemented by a book of trial liturgies, widely used by the more liberal congregations and known as *Prayer Book Studies, 30* (1990), and by publications providing the Propers for the minor "feast days." In the USA the latest edition of the traditional Prayer Book was 1928 and this was the official Book of ECUSA until it was replaced by the very different 1979 Book.

Turning to Canada we find that the latest edition of the traditional *Book of Common Prayer* was 1959/1962 and that the new book, similar to the American 1979 Book, is called *The Book of Alternative Services* (1985). Both books are used in Canada, but there is a very definite practical policy by the majority of the bishops to persuade congregations to use the new book.

In my recent published study of the new liturgies, I have attempted to show that, alongside a certain respect for the traditional services and doctrines, the recent Prayer Books contain new doctrines of the Trinity, of the Person and Work of Christ, of the nature of man and his sin, of salvation and of Scripture. Further, they show a growing readiness to use inclusive language both in the translation of sacred Scripture and in the provision of prayers and praises. For details I must invite my reader to see my book, *Proclaiming the Gospel through the Liturgy: the Common Prayer Tradition and Doctrinal Revision* (1993), along with its predecessor, *Knowing God through the Liturgy* (1992).

Perhaps I can most easily bring to the surface the new theology informing liturgical revision not only in Anglicanism, but also through the whole ecumenical movement, if I set it out in terms of "a one through five" (as I did with respect to the theology which has informed the classic Anglican Way in chapter two above). By this method, it is possible quickly and easily to compare the theological foundation of classical Anglicanism with that of much of modern Anglicanism.

The original one through five (as I set it out above in chapter two) appeared to last until recent times - the 1950s. In fact, it survived into the post World War II world in structure but not in content. Though the Bible remained the Bible with its Two Testaments, it was gradually viewed differently. It was studied via the developing historical-critical method. While this method brought benefits it also tended to make the Bible into the inspired words of men about God, rather than words inspired by God concerning God and his relation to man.

Then while the Apostles' and Nicene Creeds were retained the Nicene (with the Prefaces and Collects containing the Nicene dogma) was seen as containing what scholars were calling the "hellenization of doctrine." That is, in its presentation of the dogma of the Holy Trinity, it was judged that it contained philosophical concepts (e.g., "one substance"). Further, it was held that the onward movement of historical research raised a whole series of questions concerning the viability of building a doctrinal structure on either the theology of the Councils of the fourth and fifth cen-

turies or of the Confessions of Faith of the Reformation of
the sixteenth century.

The new 12345

Modern Anglicanism in North America (like much of
Lutheranism, Presbyterianism, Roman Catholicism and
Methodism) has intermarried with the family of theologies
we know as nineteenth-century Liberal Theology and its
modern children or developments. The children of this marriage are present everywhere in the life, witness and teaching of the Churches. What they seem to hold in common
with respect to the nature and content of worship or liturgy
is a commitment to the following: (1) Experience as the one
and only foundation; (2) Experience, however, of two kinds
- that recorded in the Bible and in Christian history and
that we enjoy today; (3) The Third Century after Christ as
the century offering most guidance to us today; (4) The benefits of four revolutions; and (5) The availability of five or
more (i.e., a plurality of) Rites for worship.

Experience - the one and only foundation. We are deal-
ing here with a very large and broad foundation. Personal
experience originates in encounter with the world, other
persons and with one's own self. Further, such experience
is continuous and so what you or I experience now is affected
in one degree or another by my previous experience of yesterday or the days before. Experience obviously includes
the various reports of the five senses as well as basic feelings,
attitudes, moods and bodily expressions. Then also there is
a common and shared experience so that people claim a
common experience and are drawn together because of it -
e.g., an association of families who have suffered and do
still suffer the pain of having lost children through drugs
and wish to help each other.

Added to direct personal experience, there is the study of
human beings as experiencing persons. Such study can be
of their inner life (psychology), their social relations and

context (sociology), of their communal practices and customs (anthropology) and of their physiological, animal state (biology). Increasingly, over the last century, experience has had the meaning of observation of facts and events as a source of knowledge.

So it is not surprising that for Liberal Christianity experience (personal, social and from empirical study) has been and is understood as a medium of disclosure about the nature of the world as well as that which is "beyond" it. Further, since experience is many-sided and multi-relational, results and findings from aesthetics as well as science, ethics as well as economics, and religious as well as secular studies are all considered.

In the most basic sense, it may be claimed that experience is the many-sided "product" of complex encounters between what there is and beings capable of undergoing, enduring, taking note of, responding to and expressing this "product." Further, such experience is the result of an ongoing process since our experiences are not isolated but are related to what has gone before. Finally, this approach to experience includes but is far more than what traditionally has been called "religious experience."

Anyone who carefully studies the new experimental services of the Episcopal Church found in *Prayer Book Studies, 30* will see how contemporary experience in the world is making its mark upon theology and worship. What used to be seen as the influence of the world, the flesh and the devil is now beginning to be seen as the presence and work of the Holy Spirit of God. One obvious example of this is the commitment of the General Convention of the Episcopal Church in August 1994 to the use of more "expansive language" (i.e., what was previously called non-excluding or inclusive language) for God and human beings in the new services.

Another example is the new general principle, so often stated at the same Indianapolis Convention, that doctrine must take into account and develop according to the actual experience of members of congregations. Therefore, for example, if a sizeable minority of members are living in "relationships" with members of the same sex, and these people find God is with them in their lives, then the doctrine of marriage and marriage services must be developed by the Church in order to take account of this primary experience.

Two Kinds of Experience - Biblical and post-biblical.
Liberal Protestantism has consistently taught that the Bible is the inspired record of the religious experience of Israel, Jesus, and the apostles of Jesus. That is, it is not (as orthodox Protestantism had claimed) the words of God in the words of men but it is rather the words of men about their experience of God. As such the Scriptures are precious and indispensable. However, the sacred books do not give us revealed teaching from God. It is the work of the contemporary theologian to use the record of the experience of God in the Old and New Testaments as the basis for his own reflection today, using the inductive and empirical method rather than the old, deductive method of pre-Enlightenment days.

As greater thought has been given to this approach since the 1960's, it has been pointed out (by feminists and others) that the experience recorded in the Bible is primarily the experience of males, written by males. In other words, it probably (certainly?) suffers from the diseases of patriarchalism, androcentricism and sexism, for it was written in a male-dominated society for the benefit of males! Therefore, it has to be studied and used with great care by those who want to produce a liberated and just society. Even so, it is valuable if for no other reason than that it is primary - for without it there would be no record of the origins of the Christian religion.

So there is biblical experience. Since the writing of the New Testament there also has been a continuing stream of what can be called "religious experience." This is recorded in a variety of sources from liturgical texts through autobiographical statements to books on prayer and spirituality. In the "holy tradition" of the Church a claimed experience of God is channeled into specific rituals (forms of worship), celebrations (festival days) and ascetic duties (e.g., the keeping of Lent). Within specific types of Christianity (e.g., Anglican, Roman Catholic, and Lutheran) there has been a specific tradition of worship and spirituality in which it has been recognized that the faithful will have had experience of God. Such religious experience is another source for theology; but, here again, there is the problem that much of it was written by males for males and from within patriarchal and racialist societies.

Thus, the claim is made today that it is necessary for the modern theologian to add to what can be learned of God from the religious experience recorded in the Bible and available through the traditions of the Church. What she or he must add is the study of experience which is not flawed through being interpreted through a patriarchalist and sexist bias. So we find that the testimony of minorities (or of women) to discrimination and deprivation becomes an important source for modern theological reflection. So it is hardly surprising that conclusions drawn from the study of selected contemporary experience are often given preference over clear teachings found in the New Testament. For example, it is often said today that a homosexual relationship is acceptable to God if the couple remain faithful to each other. Such a statement flies in the face of the teaching of both the Old and New Testaments on sexual morality, if that teaching is taken at its face value.

A few moments of reflection will lead my reader to see that once "experience" becomes the basis for theology, then there can be a spectrum of possibilities from the conservative to the radical. For example, theology can be constructed by an inductive method from:

1. The record of religious experience in the Bible.
2. The record of religious experience in the Bible and in holy tradition (or in a part thereof).
3. The record of religious experience in the Bible, Christian tradition and in the other theistic religions of the world (Islam and Judaism).
4. The record of religious experience in the Bible, Christian tradition and in all the religions of the world.

5. The record of religious experience (from all religions) and the study of the modern experience of women and/or minorities, as well as the reception of the "assured results" of study from the sociological and behavioral sciences concerning the nature and needs of human beings.

Originally, in the nineteenth century the new and learned Liberal Theology worked from (1) and (2), but in recent times such combinations as (4) and (5) have become common. That is, modern theologians tend to choose from the vast possibilities of total experience those aspects which further their position and cause.

An indication of how this approach has entered the Anglican tradition of theology is best illustrated by reference to what has often been called the three-legged stool. Since the late sixteenth century the basis of the Anglican Way has been explained in terms of a commitment to the authority of the Holy Scriptures (see numbers 1 and 2 above), to tradition (see numbers 3, 4 and 5 above), and to reason (sanctified reason seeking to make clear to any one generation what the Lord God has revealed and taught to his Church). In recent decades, there has been talk of a four-legged stool, with the fourth leg being (at first) specifically religious experience, and then being (more recently) such human experience as had bearing on modern religion. Thus instead of the Bible and traditional theology judging contemporary ideas of religion, morality and spirituality through rational study, the authority of modern experience invades and virtually takes over the exercise, and the three-legged becomes not a four-legged but in fact a one-legged stool!

The Preface to the new Canadian Anglican Prayer-Book of 1985, the *Book of Alternative Services*, tells how "experience" was a major factor in the creation of the new services. Writing in 1981 of the influences upon those who created the new American Episcopal Prayer Book of 1979, the (then) Dean of the University of the South at Sewanee, Dr. Urban T. Holmes, wrote:

> The new prayer book has, consciously or unconsciously, come to emphasize that understanding of the Christian experience which one might describe as a postcritical apprehension of symbolic reality and life in the community. It is consonant with Ricoeur's "second naiveté", and is more expressive of Husserl, Heidegger, Otto, and Rahner than Barth or Brunner. (*Worship points the Way*, 1981, p.137)

One does not need to know anything about the European philosophers and theologians on this list to gain the impression that they were not the ones supportive of traditional orthodoxy!

The Third Century. Within the Anglican Church, with its traditional Liturgy which had been in use since 1549, those who wanted to introduce theological changes through liturgy had to find a different structure for the services into which they could introduce new doctrine. However, this structure had to be from the past, and preferably from the patristic era, in order to satisfy the inherent Anglican appeal to history. Thus the appeal to the third century - an appeal which was made also by Roman Catholic scholars during and after the Second Vatican Council (1962-1965). This century was the period when the Church was in (it was claimed) the multicultural, pluralistic culture of the Roman Empire and when there was flexibility with regard to both doctrinal statements and liturgical forms. Further, this was the period when the Church was free of State control; it was not until after Constantine the Great became Emperor early in the fourth century that Christianity became a lawful and then a preferred religion of the Roman Empire. So this was the period, it was claimed, most like the modern West and thus the one to look to for inspiration!

Looking back to the Church of the third century (of which our knowledge is minimal and hazy), liturgists produced new structures for the Eucharist and then filled the structures with a mixture of traditional and modern doctrine. They were able to introduce the new teaching because, having chosen a point in history before the ecumenical councils and before the development of dogma in the fourth and fifth centuries, they were set free from that classical teaching. In his book, *Rites for a New Age* (Toronto, 1986), commending the new Canadian Prayer Book, Michael Ingham makes much of the similarity between the culture of the Roman Empire in the third and fourth centuries and that of North America today. Further, the leader of the liturgical revision in the Episcopal Church, Massey H. Shepherd Jr., wrote an essay in 1980 to point out that the 1979 Book was based on this appeal to the third century (see "The Patristic Heritage of the BCP of 1979" in *The Historical Magazine of the Protestant Episcopal Church*, Vol.53).

Four Revolutions. The theology of the new prayer books is filtered through at least four revolutions. *First,* since it is in the language of the people and is a rejection of western medieval ways, it has obviously come through the Protestant Reformation. *In the second place,* it has come through the Enlightenment of the eighteenth century for it is theology which begins with man (humankind) and works from man to God, rather than from God's self-revelation to man. It is basically a theology "from below" rather than a "theology from above." It begins from man's experience rather than from God's self-revelation.

Thirdly, it has come through that so-called liberal or modernist theology (based on experience - as explained above) which has characterized Liberal Protestantism since the beginning of the nineteenth century with the seminal work of Friedrich Schleiermacher. A careful study of the Catechism in the American 1979 Prayer Book will quickly confirm this observation that the theology has come via Liberal Theology. For example, the Catechism begins with talk of human nature (not of the self-revealing God) and there is a rejection of the doctrine of original sin (i.e., as sickness and disease of the soul) in favor of seeing sin only as the abuse of freedom. *Finally,* it has participated in the revolution which followed the Second Vatican Council. That Council opened windows through which blew a mighty gale to dislodge traditional doctrine and liturgy and make space for innovations in both theology and liturgy. (For further details I commend Klaus Gamber, *The Reform of the Roman Liturgy*, 1993.) Anyone who compares the new Anglican Liturgies with those of the Roman Catholic Church will see many similarities. Further, when the modern are compared with the pre-modern, many major differences not only of structure but also in doctrine and language will be seen.

Five Eucharistic Prayers. In the traditional *Books of Common Prayer* from 1549 to 1962 there was always only one liturgical form for the administration of the Lord's Supper, the service of Holy Communion. The point of this was to present the most excellent form possible for universal use so that there was unity not only in spirit but also in thought and words in the Church. This had the advantage that wherever the Anglican travelled and went to divine service he felt at home. In the new books, there are at least five and often more such liturgical forms. Further, there is the proviso that more such forms of service can be constructed to fit local conditions and desires.

Diversity is justified on the dubious basis that before the fourth century of the Christian era there was variety and not uniformity amongst churches. It is also justified on the basis of meeting modern needs, allowing a local congregation to choose what it thinks best serves its own, particular situation. (I may also add that diversity keeps the liturgists in business for there is, in principle, no limit to the possibilities of new forms! It also means that the principle of relativism is built into this approach to worship, for one form is said to be as good as another and what serves best is that which is *felt* to be right and appropriate in any given place at any specific time. Thereby not only the principle of excellence but also the principle of authoritative revealed doctrine is lost.)

In conclusion

Perhaps now the claim of the modern liturgical movement both in Protestantism and Roman Catholicism and through ecumenism (the World Council of Churches) that the *lex orandi* (the law of praying) is the *lex credendi* (the law of believing) can be seen for what it is. Via the new liturgies, which contain new doctrine, major changes in what the Church believes, teaches and confesses are being introduced. People are participating in the new liturgies, which still use the language of Zion, and thereby they are receiving into their minds and hearts a new theology - even perhaps a new religion. Such a route is probably a more effective route for the entrance of modernity into the liturgical churches than any other!

Modern liturgists are not, however, content merely to create the law of believing through their law of praying. They want also to proclaim that the only valid, primary theology, is theology which is based upon the liturgy - thus we hear a lot about "Liturgical Theology." Further, as the experience of the last decade has shown, the so-called liturgical theology of the "law of praying" is also easily adaptable to become the vehicle for the expression of the modern "theologies" of ecology, feminism, liberation and equal rights for any self-proclaimed, disadvantaged group.

As to the further question, "Why do these churches emphasize the Eucharist so much when they apparently do not want to make much of the sacrificial death of Jesus?"; the answer is in terms of the celebration of community. The coming together of "individuals" to form a "community of celebration" and to share a symbolic, common meal seem to be the major themes of the modern Eucharists. The emphasis is not upon the encounter with, and feeding by, the heavenly Lord Jesus Christ who comes to his people who are gathered in his name; rather it is upon the discovery of God present in and with those who come together to celebrate and affirm each other. This is why so much is made of the so-called "Peace" - the greeting of each other by hugs and handshakes. Obviously such understanding and practice harmonizes with an experiential theology (numbers 1 and 2 above).

Having set the general context of the ecumenical liturgical movement, we must now turn to look at the Rites which belong to the post-Vatican II era.

CHAPTER ELEVEN

New Rites for a New Era

The appearance of what were to become the new rites of the new Prayer Book began in the late 1960s in the ECUSA. This date is significant. It was, of course, during the sixties that American society and culture went through a massive shake-up and change of direction. Further, it was the period immediately after the Second Vatican Council, where (contrary to what was intended but as it has turned out) Roman Catholicism was allowed to flirt with, and then to enjoy, the modern world.

Liturgists, who were preparing the new Rites for the Anglican Communion of Churches, were affected to a greater or lesser degree, by the winds of change caused both by the social revolution of the 1960s and the new proposals for Liturgy advanced by Roman Catholics who were enjoying their new freedoms. Of course, not everything from the Sixties or from liberated Roman Catholicism was bad! From one came new concern for social action, and from the other came a renewed interest in the worship of the early Church. However, because of the general instability of the era in western culture and the rapid evolution (or decay) of spoken and written English, it was certainly not the period to make major, and seemingly permanent, changes in the life and worship of the Church.

Regrettably, as the new Rites began to appear, those who were producing them, as well as those who were commending them, were less than honest about their theological content. It was said over and over again from the Fifties and on into the late Sixties and throughout the Seventies, that there were no important, theological changes. The claim was that there were *only* changes in structure and language aimed at (a) making Rites more in line with ancient ones and (b) more fitting for modern man [humanity].

Honesty required

In his review article on the new ECUSA Prayer Book, the well-known Roman Catholic, Aidan Kavanagh, Professor of Liturgics at Yale, wrote: "The Book as a whole is clearly not a mere updated revision of its predecessors since 1549. It is nothing if not a new formulary that contains some structural and phraseological traces of what has gone before, but which goes quite beyond it" (*Anglican Theological Review*, vol.LVIII, p.362). In other words, it is no longer the traditional *Book of Common Prayer* even though it was given that name. Kavanagh, himself an active advocate of change, went on to say how much he appreciated the new book.

The late Urban T. Holmes of the University of the South, and a well known Episcopalian and advocate of change, was even more to the point when writing on "Theology and Religious Renewal:"

> After beginning in the 1950s with fervent protest that no theological change was to be contemplated or tolerated, the Standing Liturgical Commission (SLC) grew progressively more silent on the subject in the face of the charges by the Society for the Preservation of the Book of Common Prayer (SPBCP) that this was indeed what was happening. No matter what we may think of the SPBCP, we know that they are correct. The 1979 Book of Common Prayer indicates a notable shift in theology from the 1928 Book of Common Prayer. There is no problem with changing theology through liturgical revision; it is how Anglicans do it. But whether or not the silence of the SLC before the charges of the SPBCP was simply a matter of strategy or not, their failure to reveal to the church the theological implications of what was happening can hardly

be considered an act of reconciliation between theology and religion (*Anglican Theological Review*, Vol.LXII:1, p.13).

To this day bishops and priests of both ECUSA and the Canadian Anglican Church deny that there are any significant theological changes in the 1979 and 1985 Books. I can only think that this is because their own theological education was in a form of the conservative variety of Liberal Theology and that they equate this conservative Liberalism with classical orthodoxy.

It would certainly make for more honesty in Anglicanism if we could all agree that the new Prayer Books (whatever their strengths and weaknesses) do not belong to the family of *Books of Common Prayer*. In his much used textbook, *A History of Anglican Liturgy* (2nd ed., 1982, p.230), G. J. Cuming makes it clear that the history of the *Book of Common Prayer* ended in England when the provision of new, trial services started in 1965 (which process also ended with the provision of the *Alternative Service Book* of 1980). The same principle holds true for North America and other parts of the Anglican Communion of Churches.

I have often asked myself and others why it is that there has been such a militant attitude on behalf of some Bishops, parish priests and Deans of Seminaries in America and Canada to eliminate the use of the 1928 or 1962 Books and use only the *modern* Books or other *modern* liturgies. Various answers have crossed my mind. Maybe the new liturgies truly express their religion in which Experience has effectively replaced the Scriptures as the written word of God; perhaps they cannot bear the thought of shepherding a flock [or "a community"], who do not all eat the same grass; maybe their desire for control makes them want to make all parishes look alike, or perhaps they hate the religion of the classic *BCP*, with its emphasis upon the Majesty of God and the total sinfulness of man. Then, there is always the possibility that they recognize such things as - that the new Prayer Books make the ordination of women a possibility or reality, the adoption of a revised morality much easier, and the use of non-excluding, inclusive or expanding language the norm.

I think that the growing (and unwise) use of the word "community" for the whole denomination, as well as for the local parish, is also an important clue to the mindset of the leadership. In modern usage (which is sociological and not theological), a community is a group who share a common occupation or who come together in a voluntary way for a common purpose. The Church is therefore an association or society of "individuals" who come together for religious, social and psychological purposes. As such, in modern parlance, it is a community; and a community needs a norm or common basis to be the expression of its association and community bonding.

Once that norm is fixed, then any who do not wholly share it become a threat to this community! They have to be brought to conformity or pushed out. Further, because the ECUSA and Anglican Church in Canada are more to the left than the right in social and political activities, then the community will tolerate experiments on the left (e.g., further inclusive language and rites for homosexual marriages), but will not readily allow the use of a traditional rite (the 1928 BCP or the Missal) on the right!

The Structure and Contents of the New Rites

The primary division in the new rites in the 1979 Book (as well as the Canadian 1985) is between Part One, which is called, "The Word of God," and Part Two, which is called, "The Holy Communion." This division is imposed even upon Rite I which contains a conservative revision (Eucharistic Prayer I) and a radical revision (Eucharistic Prayer II) of the 1928 text (i.e., of the traditional American, Episcopal Eucharistic Service since 1789). In adopting this structure and these contents, liturgists of the Anglican Communion essentially followed the general path of the post-Vatican II Rites. One practical effect of it has been to give excessive emphasis to "The Peace" at the center, in terms of people greeting one another. (In the old Latin Rite, in the Missal, and in the Canadian 1959/1962 BCP, the "Peace" is after the Prayer of Consecration, as people kneel.)

Liturgists were particularly interested in taking third or fourth-century models for their work. Frequent mention is made, for example, in liturgical studies of Hippolytus of Rome and his work known as *The Apostolic Tradition*, which dates from the early third century. Eucharistic Prayer D in Rite II is intended as a modern rendering of a Prayer originally composed by St Basil (d.379) and now found in the Greek Liturgy. Anyone who studies with great care the original Prayer and the modern rendering of it, will gain great insight into the way modern liturgists (Roman and Protestant) develop ancient texts. Put simply, they simplify them by the use of a mindset and methods based on Liberal Theology.

The content of Part One of the new Rites, which has certain flexibility, is as follows:

The Opening Acclamation
The Collect for Purity
The Law (Rite I)
The *Gloria in Excelsis* or other Song of Praise
The *Kyrie* or *Trisagion*
The Collect
The Lessons - the O.T., the Epistle and the Gospel
The Sermon
The Nicene Creed
The Prayers of the People
The Confession of Sin
The Absolution
(The Sentences of Scripture)
The Peace

The content of Part Two, which provides for a variety of Eucharistic Prayers, is as follows:

The Offertory Sentences
The Preparation of the Table and the Presentation of the Offerings
The Great Thanksgiving

The *Sursum Corda*
The *Sanctus*
The *Benedictus qui venit*
The Institution Narrative
The Memorial Acclamation
The *Anamnesis*
The *Epiclesis*
The Supplications
The Doxology
The People's *Amen*
The Lord's Prayer
The Breaking of Bread & Fraction Anthem
The Prayer of Humble Access (Rite I only)
The Administration of Communion
The Postcommunion Prayer
The Blessing

While the rubrics of the Rite I and Rite II assume that the priest will face the altar while praying "The Great Thanksgiving," it has become the commonly accepted pattern for the priest to go behind the altar and face the people.

Facing the people for the whole of "The Great Thanksgiving" is based upon a recent theory of liturgists and made into a fixed rule by many bishops and parish priests, even though there is an abundance of historical evidence which contradicts it. The authentic or normal way of celebration is towards the East, to face the rising sun which is the symbol both of the resurrection of Jesus Christ and of his coming again in glory. The facing of the people is advocated because it is the best position if the eucharistic assembly is seen as "the gathering of the community" where everyone can see everyone! (See further Klaus Gamber, *The Reform of the Roman Liturgy*, Part II.)

There is no doubt but that the facing of the people (the Westward, in contrast to the Eastward and Northward) has occurred because of the document, *Instruction on the Liturgy* issued by the Vatican Sacred Congregation of Rites, on October 16, 1964. In chapter five we read:

> It is proper that the main altar be constructed separately
> from the wall, so that one may go around it with ease and

so that celebration may take place facing the people; it shall occupy a place in the sacred building which is truly central, so that the attention of the whole congregation of the faithful is spontaneously turned to it (para.91).

Those who have been Roman Catholics, or are familiar with Roman Catholic churches, will know the great pain felt by thousands of Catholics at the implementation of this advice.

Already the name of Hippolytus has been mentioned. The Englishman, Gregory Dix, did much to make the work of Hippolytus widely known. He also introduced liturgists to his theory of "the four-action shape of the Liturgy." In his very readable and most influential book, *The Shape of the Liturgy*, Dix laid it down (as if it were as sure as two and two make four) that there are four moments of the Eucharist - the Offertory (the bread and wine taken and placed on the altar), The Prayer (= the Great Thanksgiving), the Fraction (the bread is broken), and the Communion (the bread and wine are distributed together). Such was the ancient way, Dix maintained, and it had been lost but was recoverable.

It has been observed by Kenneth Stevenson that,

The influence of this four-fold action shape on liturgical revision has been immense. It could almost be said that every rite that has been compiled since manifests the work of Dix as its revised structure, and this does not apply simply to new rites, it also applies to old rites which are re-arranged to make their "shape" clearer (*Gregory Dix 25 Years on*, 1977, p.24).

The American 1979 Book and the Canadian 1985 Book fit into this description. Their construction around the four-fold shape is obvious. In fact, the American liturgist, Leonel L. Mitchell, wrote that, although he believed Dix's work had been nuanced by further scholarship, he also affirmed that Dix's analysis of the four-fold shape of the liturgy is correct (*Praying Shapes Believing*, 1979, pp.146-147). Many other teachers of liturgy have echoed what Mitchell believed and Dix's *Shape* has had a wide sale.

In fact, scholarship has shown that Dix was wrong in his dogmatic assertion of the four-fold shape (and this is one reason why some liturgists want to revise many current modern-language liturgies which are based on this theory). Bishop Colin Buchanan expressed the state of affairs well when he wrote:

> "Dix's role is not that of a high-profile but perverse theologian who needs to be cut down to size...it is rather that of a beacon which has consciously or unconsciously led a whole fleet astray, and our task is to get the fleet on course" (*The End of the Offertory*, 1978, p.29).

What seems clear to me (and many others) is that there is a two-fold basic action - that of blessing/giving thanks [He blessed or gave thanks] and of giving [He gave]. There is a legitimate variety of ways of setting this basic two-fold action within a Rite as the various editions of the *Book of Common Prayer* (e.g. 1549, 1662 and 1928) illustrate. But making too much of the Offertory or of the Fraction is to major on minors! Liturgists were quite wrong to force the classic text of the *BCP* into the Dix mold for the "Traditional Rite" of the new Books! They were also to wrong to treat the Dix mold as dogmatic for their new rites!

On making the New acceptable

For those who are aware of the theological trends of the new Books, there is much useful material and helpful insights within them. So they can be a useful resource for those who know how to read them. However, to use them uncritically, and as if they were theologically wholly acceptable by orthodox standards, is a mistake.

As a temporary way forward for those who are using the modern Rites of the American or Canadian Prayer Books and who wish to be faithful to Scripture and Tradition, I suggest the following corrections to the 1979 and 1985 Rites to make them right. There is no way of making the latest set of Rites (e.g. in *Prayer Book Studies 30*) right by orthodox criteria. In the present state of the American Episcopal Church (following the General Convention of 1994), where "each man [bishop] does what is right in his own eyes" (at least with regard to teaching sexual morality), it is appropriate for traditional Anglicans to fine-tune the official liturgies in order to make them speak for dynamic orthodoxy and thus to honor and glorify the Father through the Son and by the Holy Spirit. Here are my suggestions.

(a) Use only the traditional translation of the Nicene Creed which begins with "I believe..." and which speaks of the Lord Jesus Christ as being "of one substance with the Father." The modern "We believe..." form is a dishonest translation intended to allow for the inclusion of modern, liberal doctrines. Further, though the Fathers at the Councils of Nicea and Constantinople did say "We..." together, the Creed became the Baptismal Creed of the East and entered the Liturgy as such - thus "I believe..."

(b) In line with the classic, orthodox way of addressing and speaking of the Blessed, holy and undivided Trinity, revise the modern way of saying, "God: Father, Son and Holy Spirit" which appears in many places in both 1979 and 1985. This new way is deliberately designed to allow for a variety of approaches to the concept of God as Three. Its obvious meaning in terms of its punctuation is that the one God has three names or three natures. In contrast, the classical way, which speaks of "the Name of the Father, and of the Son, and of the Holy Spirit," is both biblical and patristic and much preferable. Thus the opening greeting could be as with the Greek Liturgy: "Blessed be the kingdom of the Father and the Son and the Holy Spirit, now and always, even unto ages of ages." Or if done with a response: "Blessed be God, the Father, the Son and the Holy Spirit," with the response, " And blessed be his kingdom, now and forever. Amen."

(c) Examine all Prefaces and Collects used - especially those in the other official books which provide Collects and Readings for the growing number of saints remembered in the Episcopal calendar - to make sure that they are faithful in expression to classic orthodoxy. (If in doubt go back to pre-Vatican II Roman Catholic sources or to good translations of Greek Orthodox Liturgies to check the right way to address the Blessed Trinity.)

(d) Make sure, by the addition of words where necessary, that the Great Thanksgiving is specifically addressed to "the Father." True Christian prayer is to the Father through the Son and in the Spirit. Modern use of the 1979 and 1985 Prayer Books (influenced by what is very obvious in the new Rites of *Prayer Book Studies, 30*) is often so done as to minimize the use of the revealed name of "the Father." At the General Convention of the ECUSA in Indianapolis 1994 the major Eucharist on Sunday was of this kind. In this celebration of the ministry of women (where virtually nothing was said of women as wives and mothers) there was an obvious reluctance to name "the Father," and a preference to address God in terms which allowed for a variety of concepts of God from pantheism through panentheism and Deism to Unitarianism.

(e) Beware of inclusive language in the Psalter, in the Hymn Book and in Canticles. Use the RSV or the NEB (not the NRSV or REB) for the Psalter. Or go for the 1928 Psalter! The Psalter in the new Prayer Books (as the Psalms in the new Bible translations) is according to inclusive or expansive language. This prevents the Psalter being prayed "in and with Christ in his Church." (See e.g., Psalm 1 where "he" [Christ] has become "they.")

(f) Restore the ancient "and with your spirit" instead of "and also with you." And make the Peace to be dignified and in tune with the spirit of Christ - not a free-for-all greeting as occurs at the airport gate when absent friends/relatives are greeted in a fulsome way!

(g) Carefully look at the appointed readings of the Lectionary and do not leave out those verses which teach "hard truths." Also be aware of what is deliberately left out of the modern Lectionary - e.g., teaching on the divine order for marriage and the sinfulness of practicing homosexuality and lesbianism.

(h) Amend "Christ our Passover is sacrificed for us" in order to avoid any suggestion of the medieval notion of the re-presentation of the one Sacrifice of Calvary. This can be done in one of two possible ways. First, use a sound translation of I Corinthians 5:7 ["Christ our paschal Lamb has been sacrificed. Let us, therefore, celebrate the festival..."] Secondly, use the full words of 1549 ["Christ our paschal Lamb is offered up for us, once for all, when he bare our sins on his own body upon the cross, for he is the very Lamb of God that taketh away the sins of the world: wherefore let us keep a joyful and holy feast with the Lord"].

(i) Do not be bound in the celebration of the holy Sacrament by the theories of Gregory Dix and his disciples - e.g., do not make the Offertory into a big thing and do not make the Fraction into more than it ought to be.

(j) Obey the rubrics and celebrate Eastward. The Celebrant is described in these words - "Then, facing the Holy Table, the Celebrant proceeds..."

(k) Always preach a sound, biblically-based sermon which is truly a proclamation of the Gospel and a challenge to the hearers to follow Jesus Christ and to walk in the Spirit in a manner pleasing to the heavenly Father.

(l) Seek to keep an ordered relation between the Daily Office and the Eucharist. On Sundays make sure that the Daily Office is said in the church and keep on reminding people that it is said, and that they are invited!

(m) Pray God to help to preserve in modern worship *a great sense of his majestic transcendence* as well as his gracious immanence.

I suspect that as the liberal elements within the ECUSA press on to more inclusive, expansive liturgies and thus away from classic orthodoxy that it will be easier to reform the 1979 Book in a traditional, biblical and orthodox direction. (See further my *Proclaiming the Gospel through the Liturgy,* for a study of the doctrinal innovations of the new Books.)

CHAPTER TWELVE

Guidelines

In the supermarket of American religion and its Anglican department, one opinion is usually judged as good as another. So what I have to say is obviously my opinion and the opinion of an alien at that - a legally resident alien.

First of all, I believe that the study of the history of Anglicanism makes reasonably clear that there are in essence three types of Rite for Holy Communion. The first and the most common one is that of the 1552/1559/1604/1662 Books. This has the Prayer of Consecration, containing the words of Institution, as its center. It is a simplification of the Western Rite in the light of the biblical and pastoral concerns of the Reformation. The second is that of the 1637/1762/1789/1928 Books of Scotland and America. This is an attempt to take the essentials of the Eastern Rites and make sure that the Anglican Rite has them. In this sense it is anti-Roman. It contains the Memorial, the Invocation and the Oblation all in the one prayer. Finally, there is the third, the way of the Missal, which is to add to the Anglican Rite from the pre-Vatican II Roman Rite, so that it looks like the latter, and is unmistakably Western. Between the three types are variations of them (e.g., the taking of a little from the Missal for use with the 1662 and 1928 Rites, and the Eucharistic Prayer of the Canadian 1959/1962 Book).

The new Rites of the new Prayer Books of the Anglican Communion contain a new type - the ecumenical or post-Vatican II type. This Order can be filled with sound, ortho-dox doctrine, ceremonial and devotion, but even when this occurs (and it is becoming rare) it is not Anglican. In the supermarket of religion it is a "generic" product; thus it has no distinctiveness as a particular or unique means of the worship and service of Almighty God, the Father of our Lord Jesus Christ. The Anglican Way claims to exist as a small part of the One Church of God seeking unity without uni-formity. Even as there are seven colors to the rainbow, with each color being a genuine color but the seven as one being the rainbow, so there is unity without uniformity in the one, holy, catholic and apostolic Church. Aspects of the modern ecumenical movement seem to exist to crush genuine vari-ety in the search for uniformity.

Therefore, *in the second place*, I think that there is or ought to be a legitimate variety and limited comprehen-siveness to Anglicanism as a movement and as a Commun-ion of Churches. In other words, Anglicanism is wide enough to embrace the low-church evangelical, who uses the 1662 *BCP*, the high-church catholic, who uses the Missal, based upon the *BCP*, and the one who uses the new Service Books in as near an orthodox way as possible. This means that the movement called the Anglican Way tolerates a variety of views of the Eucharistic Presence, the Eucharistic Offer-ing, Ceremonial and Vestments, not to mention devotional practices. Also it accepts the "extras" of charismatic wor-ship, even as it accepts the extras of the Missal, and the free prayers of the evangelicals! There are too few of us to be divided where we need not be!

However, this width must also have depth and this en-tails, I think, a commitment to what is known either as the Chicago or Lambeth Quadrilateral - the four principles being: (1) the Holy Scriptures as containing all things nec-essary to salvation; (2) the Apostles' and Nicene Creeds; (3) the two Sacraments ordained by Christ himself, Baptism and the Supper of the Lord; and (4) the Historic Episco-pate, locally adapted according to the varying needs of na-tions and peoples. The last principle means in practice that only episcopally ordained *men* ought to serve in the Anglican Communion of Churches as bishops and priests.

I look forward to the day when Bishops of the official Anglican Communion, who see themselves as upholding the four principles, will be in communion with Bishops of the Continuing Anglican Churches and of the Reformed Episcopal Church, even as the latter are in communion one with another. There is a great need for such communion and it will come about as all draw nearer to the Head of the Body, even our Lord Jesus Christ. It will not happen overnight but we ought to work towards it.

In the third place, I think that there is an open door within American society for any authentic form of Anglicanism, which is evangelistic and warm hearted and whose liturgy is immediately recognized as being a meeting-point between the Lord and his Church. A dignified liturgy, both evangelical and catholic, in which heaven descends in the Spirit or the congregation ascends to heaven in the Spirit, is surely what many people desire and strive for - even if they do not articulate it as I have just done. Of course, in saying this I am assuming that the congregation with the fine liturgy is seeking to be holy as God is holy and is as a light set upon a hill which cannot be hidden in terms of morality and spirituality. An Anglican congregation will not normally grow as fast as a typical American independent or community church because it is much more counter-cultural in its whole ethos and content. But growth there will be, caused by both simple evangelism (gossiping the Gospel and telling the Truth to one's neighbors and workmates) and by the sheer attractiveness of an other-worldly form of worship.

So much modern liturgical worship in Roman Catholicism and Episcopalianism has lost the sense of Majesty and awe as its users have searched for relevance and "community." The result is that so many people are unfulfilled spiritually, aesthetically and are lacking sufficient sense of the transcendent, holy, Lord God. Therefore, the need is there even with church-going people for classic, high-quality Anglican worship where there is that appropriate experience of the living God in both his transcendent and his immanent presence.

In the fourth place, I think that we ought to maintain and teach the close connexion between the Eucharist and the Daily Office. For example, the full Sunday morning at church for enthusiastic Anglicans could be Morning Prayer or Matins, followed by Sunday School, followed by Holy Communion. Alternatively, Morning Prayer and Holy Communion could be united. The point of this is to ensure that the church does not forget that a basic principle of the Anglican Way is the offering to God of *daily* worship, praise, thanksgiving, petition, intercession, and confession, and that this occurs also on Sunday as well. Hopefully, the Daily Office, either in the morning or the evening or both, will be prayed each day by the priest and any others who are free to come (as well as by all members in spirit wherever they are).

At least, it ought to be possible for a parish to make sure that all members are given the opportunity to read the Bible according to an agreed Lectionary. If any Bible Studies occur in the parish, it is also good that they be linked to either the Daily or the Sunday Lectionary. No Lectionary is perfect and some are better than others, but the first priority is actually to choose one and to stick to it long enough to appreciate the spiritual value of a lectionary.

In the fifth place, there is a very important pastoral need for the Sunday worship to have the same liturgical structure and content on each Lord's Day and major Festival. Of course there will be changes of season and different Bible Readings, Collects, Prefaces, Psalms and Hymns. However, the ability to worship through a written Liturgy depends both upon a person growing into it and the liturgy growing into the person. Such a two way growth takes time and it is stunted and harmed by swopping and changing the Rite. Innovation and surprise are not a part of the Anglican Way! The modern yearning for novelty ought not to intrude into holy Liturgy!

This said, I can see that where a mature priest celebrates the Holy Communion daily with only a few people in attendance, then a certain variety of the use of Rites and variation within Rites could occur and be beneficial. Maybe it is on such occasions that the 1549 and the 1764 Rites could be helpful.

In the sixth place, there is need to be aware of being taken in by fads, novelties and pressures, which have nothing to do in essence with the worship of God the Father Almighty. These may be with respect to vestments, music, ceremonial, "the peace," or one of many other things. What we have to do in the use of a Rite, we need to do well. This means doing well both the preparation for, and the celebration of a liturgy; all of which, can be very demanding. There is no need, I believe, to be writing ever more new liturgies. We shall never be able to write a perfect Rite but what we can do, by God's grace, is to seek to perfect our use of a Rite, which has deep biblical and theological roots and content, to his glory and our good.

There is possibly a need to put into good, modern English the older Rites such as 1662 and 1928. Before doing this and using such a service, I think that we need to be clear that this is truly what will help people draw near to God. Spiritually speaking there are distinct advantages today in using older English - e.g., the different language helps us to realize that we are in a holy place for a holy purpose, and the use of the old second person singular makes clear the personal relation between the baptized, believing Christian and his Lord.

In conclusion and in summary, I have tried in this short book to introduce to my reader the orthodox Rites for Holy Communion of Anglicanism in North America and to suggest their meaning and their usage. There are many things I have not said but could have said - e.g., of adding suitable extra material for special days. However, when any one of these Rites, which I have commended, is used according to its own internal logic and spirituality, it becomes by the gracious kindness of the Father, the mediatorial work of Jesus Christ, the Son, and the action of the Holy Spirit a means whereby our wholeselves - body, mind and spirit - are engaged in the worship of the Father through the Son by the Spirit. Since we are created to enjoy and glorify the Lord our God, then we can ask for nothing higher than this - the privileged opportunity to enjoy and glory our heavenly Father in the holy Eucharist as we are fed in the Spirit by the Body and Blood of the Incarnate Son.

Epilogue

To commend religious products of the seventeenth (the 1662 *BCP*) and eighteenth (the *Scottish Office* and thus the 1928 *BCP*) centuries brings forth the charge of living in the past - of being out of touch and out of date. After all, are not all the Prayer Books commended in the chapters of this book products of the pre-modern age, and certainly of the pre-post-modern age? Such is the kind of question asked of, and charged by both modern liturgists, who have a big investment in change and development, and regular churchgoers, who have got used to modern life.

Is there an answer to the question? Yes, I think that there is! And here is a sketch of one way of providing it.

Towards an answer

First of all, it is appropriate to ask whether or not (after all the millions of dollars spent on the expenses of the Liturgical Commissions and the printing costs for various form of trial liturgies, not to mention the great emotional strain of all the experimentation) we have been given products which are spiritually and theologically superior to the older ones. That is, in terms of bringing people to the Lord our God in humble, reverential and authentic worship, do the post-1960's Rites actually perform this task in a markedly superior way to the older Rites? Is their *lex orandi* superior to that of the older Rites?

To these questions some will immediately answer "yes," because they believe that the use of modern language forms for modern people is necessary or at least very helpful. Traditional language is a barrier, they say. Such people making this claim must then, I think, honestly face this question: Have you ever tried the classic Rites in a modernized English? And here the answer is usually "No," because the modern liturgists have not provided such a possibility. As we have seen, their modern English Rites are based on very recent theories and theologies of what is the proper structure and content of an Order of worship.

However, if we take a look at the Orthodox Church in its various forms and jurisdictions, we find that the ancient Liturgy has not been changed or revised or upgraded. Further, in terms of the type of English used, the bishops allow both traditional and contemporary translations of the Greek original. So here the modern language version is the vehicle for a Liturgy, which was produced in the early centuries of the Church. Modern English does not mean a modernized service! And, as far as I can tell, this Church is growing quickly in America.

Other people will answer "yes" to the question concerning the superiority of contemporary forms, because they believe that the human soul is different in expression (if not in content) today than it was in pre-modern times. It is often argued that pastors and liturgists have to take very seriously the fact of obvious introspection and absorption with feelings, individualism, sense of alienation and felt need of community, especially in the city with its suburbia. Gone are the ordered classes of society, the extended families and the sense of belonging to a fixed group.

Further, it is said that we must recognize that we do not have (and, in fact, ought not to have) that sense of sinfulness and separation from God which medieval and early modern (16th-18th centuries) folks had. Modern people do not think of God, it is claimed, as the high and holy One, who sees our human wretchedness and sinfulness and calls us to go for cleansing to the Blood of Christ! Rather, today people feel the need for a God who is present in and with us, the God of Creation and of Nature. They desire to celebrate God's presence in the world as much as (if not more than) in the great saving deeds of history, via the pages of the Bible, and in holy tradition. Their hope is to be affirmed before a loving God, whose compassion is like that of a caring mother, not thrown down into the dust before a holy, wrathful, patriarchal Judge.

There is some truth to this way of stating the felt needs of people in the pews today. However, that "some truth" in this context can probably be faced, pastorally met and provided for, by the context and ethos of services, the quality of the fellowship in Christ, and the content of sermons, teaching, and writings. Further. what are deemed to be (after due consideration) any weaknesses of the older Rites (e.g., lacking both a distinct missionary/evangelistic vision and a vivid recognition of God's presence in his world) can easily be put right in the use of occasional collects/prayers, in church programs, and sermons, for example.

Three options

It may be said that there are three possibilities before us. *One* is the way of *archaism*. Here the older Rites are used as fossils from the past, as signs of a dead conservatism, and as an escape from the horrors of the modern world. I am sure that there are people who use the Missal, the 1662 and the 1928 Books in this way. Where they do this there is no growth in numbers or quality because fossils cannot grow. On the other hand, a few people of like mind will probably be attracted and thus this approach will continue as long as there is conservatism in the culture.

Another way, which seems to be dominant in the Episcopal Church and the Anglican Church of Canada today, is that of *futurism*. Because of its own style and thought-forms, the way into the past is closed off for modernity, and so the only way is into the future. The few controls for this journey seem to be those brought from the past into the present. Yet, in comparison with the pull of the future, these controls are weak. Thus, in practice, as we see in the work of liturgical commissions and in the agenda being placed before them, as well as in a growing number of very public liturgies at Conventions and Conferences, the move is always into new territory - inclusive or expansive language services and new rites for new situations (e.g., the blessing of a same-sex marriage). The new Prayer Books from 1979 onwards are the beginnings of the liturgical expression of futurism. The liturgical movement has to keep on going on, for to go on is its only way to be true to itself.

The third way, and the way commended in this book, is *realism*. The Lord our God, he is our Father and we, by the grace of our Lord Jesus Christ and through the sanctifying presence of the Holy Spirit, are his adopted children. As such we are called to worship the Father in spirit and in truth as the Family of God, the Body of Christ and the Bride of Christ. One, well-tested and well-tried way to do so is that of Anglican *Common Prayer*. Of course, this way is not perfect: the only perfect liturgy is that of the angels and saints in heaven. However, it is, in its imperfections, an established and authentic way. Indeed, it is an excellent way. The new liturgical products, because of their inherent instability through partaking of futurism, cannot provide an assured, authentic worship today for faithful souls. So we turn to the Common Prayer tradition and we receive it thankfully.

Realism means the receiving of the living past for the present and on into the future under the confession, "Jesus Christ is Lord." Therefore, it is not to be confused with archaism or futurism. We use it to worship the Blessed, Holy and Undivided Trinity, the Lord our God, who is the same yesterday, today and forever. In his holy service, the past is the living past. It is the way of faith, hope, and charity.

In the older Rites (in contrast to the new ones) there is a vivid sense of both the majestic, holy transcendence and the glorious, comforting immanence of the living God. Further, the presence of God in his world and in his Church is, of necessity, dependent upon and secondary unto his presence unto himself in his glorious Trinitarian Being, outside all space and time, and beyond all infinity and eternity. For

God is the Creator who made the cosmos out of nothing; thus God without his world remains truly God unto himself! In contrast, in pantheism God minus the world is nothing at all! So we cry out, "Let God be God!"

For Further Reading

The First and Second Prayer Books of Edward VI, in the Everyman Edition, New York, 1952.
The Two Liturgies with other Documents set forth by Authority in the Reign of King Edward VI, The Parker Society, Cambridge, 1844.

C. J.Cocksworth, *Evangelical Eucharistic Thought in the Church of England,* Cambridge, 1993.
G. J.Cuming, *A History of Anglican Liturgy,* 2nd.ed., London, 1982.
Gordon Donaldson, *The Making of the Scottish Prayer Book of 1637,* Edinburgh, 1954.
John Dowden, *The Scottish Communion Office 1764,* ed., H. A.Wilson, Oxford, 1922.
Klaus Gamber, *The Reform of the Roman Liturgy,* San Juan Capistrano, 1993.
W. J.Grisbrooke, *Anglican Liturgies of the 17th and 18th Centuries,* London, 1958.
A. C.Guelzo, *For the Union of Evangelical Christendom. The Irony of the Reformed Episcopalians,* University Park, Pa., 1994.

Samuel Hart, *Bishop Seabury's Communion Office*, New York, 1893.

M. J.Hatchett, *A Commentary on the American Prayer Book*, New York, 1980.

R. C. D.Jasper, *The Development of the Anglican Liturgy, 1662-1980*, London, 1989.

R. C. D.Jasper & G.J.Cuming, *Prayers of the Eucharist, Early and Reformed*, 2nd.ed., London, 1980.

A. J. MacDonald, *The Evangelical Doctrine of Holy Communion*, Cambridge, 1930.

Charles Neil & J.M. Willoughby, *The Tutorial Prayer Book*, London, 1913.

E. C. Ratcliff, *Liturgical Studies*, London, 1976.

M. H.Shepherd, *The Oxford American Prayer Book Commentary*, New York, 1950.

Bard Thompson, *Liturgies of the Western Church*, Philadelphia, 1961.

Peter Toon, *Knowing God through the Liturgy*, Largo, Florida, 1992.

Peter Toon, *Proclaiming the Gospel through the Liturgy*, Largo, Florida, 1993.

[The last two are available from The Prayer Book Society Publishing House, P.O. Box 268, Largo. Florida 34649. Phone 813-596-6212]

Index of Names

WHO IS PRESERVATION PRESS?
by Jim Whitacre

Preservation Press is a publisher of classic Christian titles, as well as, other titles that support classic Christian thought and practice. This organization was created as a response to the inferior moral character of our modern culture. We live in troubling times. The fabric of society that once was sewn together with the thread of Christian values set forth under God's law has now been frayed and torn by the insidious guise of social tolerance under man's law. Morality, or lack of, was once very easily discerned because the foundation of society was rooted in traditional Christianity. Today, the word tradition falls into the politically incorrect category; values and moral character are borne out of whatever happens to be the latest psycho-social theory in vogue. There is a stark contrast between truth based on the revelation of God, and modern thinking which is based solely on "individual feelings" gained through "the human experience". In other words, modernity has become an enemy of the Cross of Christ, making God its belly (Philippians 3:18, 19). There was once a day when this was simply recognized for what it is; sin and idolatry. True spirituality, true Christianity is evidenced by our repentant response to the revelation of God by turning from "dead idols" to serve the "living and true God" (1 Thessalonians 1:9).

In response to the tumult of the day, Preservation Press is committed to the restoration of classic Christian thinking. We have recognized that there is a marked decline in publishers who concentrate on traditional Christian work, but rather publish works that appeal to the modern way of thinking. This creates, therefore, a tedious job of book selection for those who desire classic Christian reading. Preservation Press has made a conscious decision to promote literature that proclaims the classic Christian position: The Trinitarian God, who is God in and unto Himself; revealing Himself to us in and through His Son, Jesus Christ, in both Word and Sacrament; by and with the Holy Spirit.

It is our hope that you will support us in the effort to turn the hearts and minds of those both within and without the Church, that the peace of Christ might reign.